THE ABCs OF
DIVERSITY

A MANAGER'S GUIDE TO DIVERSITY, EQUITY, AND INCLUSION IN THE NEW WORKPLACE

MARTINE KALAW

ISBN (Paperback): 978-1-950336-25-8
ISBN (eBook): 978-1-950336-24-1

Published by BestsellingBook.com

Table of Contents

Introduction

In my career, I've had a number of bosses — maybe about ten. Half were men, and four out of those five were white. And all of them, consistently and across four different industries would ask me, "Is anyone bothering you? Are you okay? Because if anyone's bothering you, you have to let me know."

I always appreciated it. It was like I had big brothers looking after me, especially in my first few months with a company. But I never considered the pattern or consistency of those questions until recently. I'm sure if I were to ask them what drove those questions, they would probably say, "Oh, I was just making sure you were okay."

But somewhere subconsciously, I believe that they could observe the lack of diversity in one or several categories within their organization and wanted to look out for me: a black woman. We, as managers, are much more self-aware and see more than we care to admit.

Again, I appreciated it so much. They had brought me onto their teams and wanted to make me feel safe and valued there. That speaks volumes about their character. But taking a step back and looking at these questions through a different lens, that was one of the most direct ways that my bosses addressed diversity issues and it wasn't very direct at all.

And other organizations are in a similar situation — people know that a lack of diversity is a problem in their companies, but they don't have the vocabulary, or tools, to address it head-on.

Events like the tragic death of George Floyd have our society openly discussing diversity in its many forms, whether it's around race, gender, nationality, sexuality or any other marginalized identity. And along with that comes attempted conversations about diversity, equity, and inclusion (DEI) in the workplace.

Companies feel pressure to publicly address what's happening in the world, but end up taking steps that actually hurt them in the long run. Senior management isn't sure how to facilitate dialogue with their employees about DEI, nor do they see how diversity, or lack thereof, plays out on a day-to-day basis within their company.

This lack of fruitful conversation around diversity doesn't just affect Human Resources (HR) or how a company is perceived on social media, it has sweeping effects for everyone in a company. People in marginalized groups might not trust that their contributions are as valued as everyone else's and may leave their position if they feel alienated. We might not realize that our unconscious biases are lowering our team's morale and driving away great talent or if we are aware of our personal privilege, we might not know how to be a good ally to our team.

We can't afford to rely on indirect (though well-intentioned) conversations or top-down methods of reacting to DEI issues that are thrown our way. Change can come from the middle — middle management, specifically. We should, and can be, the driving force for DEI initiatives because we have more influence than we realize.

Think about it — senior leadership doesn't really have the capacity, time, or bandwidth to interact with individual contributors on a day-to-day basis, so they rely on middle management to translate whatever the experiences entry level employees have.

Middle management's influence is even more visible when it comes to mid- and entry-level employees. No one can motivate or de-motivate someone quite like their boss, as we'll discuss further in chapter two. Employees often have the longest standing relationships with their managers, more so than even their co-workers, who come and go. If an employee has to interact with someone who delivers microaggressions to them regularly, or makes them feel like they're a less valued member of a team, they probably won't work to their fullest potential.

But if that same employee works with a manager who's aware of their unconscious biases and is willing to be an active ally, the employee will feel safe and comfortable — like they belong. They won't leave to find a job where they think they'll be more valued, so they'll be able to reach their potential in their current role.

In short, they'll be much happier and more secure, which is not only good for them, but it's good for the company's productivity.

After reading all of this so far, you're probably wondering where I drew these conclusions from, or why I'm so passionate about empowering middle managers to drive change within their organizations, or why I'm writing this book at all.

I decided to write this book because I was scared of going to work for almost six months straight.

I felt the same way I did in my middle school days when I never wanted to go to school because I was bullied. And here I was — a 30-something-year-old woman who was a mid-level manager at a prestigious organization, and I felt the same way as I did back then.

Simply put, I was scared to go to work because I felt different. I was one of two Black women and three Black people in the entire organization, so I felt like people either saw only my Blackness or they didn't see me because of my Blackness.

There was so much pressure to perform and seem overly energetic so that people would not know how I really felt deep down inside or put me in the box of "angry black woman," and so I grappled with this gnawing fear and anxiety every day for six months.

Soon it occurred to me that I could not belong in this organization because I just didn't feel welcomed or included. It completely affected my performance and I know I'm not the only person who isn't a part of the majority who has felt this way.

When I became a middle manager and eventually went on to develop management training, I realized that I had the power to combine my unique perspective with the strengths of middle management to enhance diversity, equity, and inclusion within organizations.

I've lived in so many worlds, figuratively and literally speaking. Though I was born in Zambia, my family is from the Democratic Republic of Congo, and I moved to the US when I was four years old. Within the US, I've lived in international communities and predominantly white communities, and I went to both predominantly African American schools and a boarding school that was a mix of southern white kids and international students from all over. I was undocumented and stateless after my mother and stepfather passed, which exposed me to a whole other group of individuals to identify with.

This unique perspective allows me to pivot and see things from viewpoints that I don't know that the average person would need to or have to see. It's allowed me to look beyond myself and have empathy and compassion for various communities, including my own. These experiences have been invaluable in developing the content of this book and in my seminars on DEI in the workplace.

The tools and stories within this book will empower you to approach DEI without fear of saying the wrong thing or feeling personally attacked so you can build (or re-build) trust within your team. Instead of shying away from hard conversations about our unconscious biases or microaggressions, you'll be able to take them on and be an active ally to the people you manage.

I've compiled a list of steps you can take and phrases you can use the next time someone says something to offend you, or when you are accused of offending someone. Rather than shy away from DEI dialogue, my checklist equips you with the confidence to engage in conversation, listen and be heard, and build relationships, regardless of who you are. You can find that resource by clicking the link, or going to the following URL: martinekalaw.com/checklist.

You'll also learn about your own blind spots and gain the confidence to lead your team knowing that everyone feels welcomed. As a result, the entire company will see the benefits of increased diversity — more satisfied employees, better problem-solving, and better productivity.

I come across articles practically daily that profess that DEI initiatives are ineffective. Some argue that DEI training can be more damaging because when people feel forced to make change, they are more likely to retaliate.

I agree with these arguments, but I need to also highlight the underlying issue. We don't make DEI accessible or approachable to the people who have the ability to make the most impact. Instead, DEI can seem exclusive and only available to the few who might have studied something like *Critical Race Theory* in graduate school.

We, as middle managers, can change that perception. We can shift the way that the workforce approaches diversity, equity, and inclusion, making it accessible for all. We have the power to unify people, to understand each other, and to see how our differences make us who we are. As a manager, you have the ability to do something that many organizations are struggling to do, creating change that will sweep across the country and the world.

Training can have a positive impact on DEI, but it has to be in conjunction with actions. Actions and initiatives are only as effective as the strategy behind them. All organizations should equip managers with access to affect DEI – that is the only strategy that will further DEI.

My goal in writing this book is to make DEI accessible to everyone within an organization, especially hiring managers. While conversations around DEI are not easy, they shouldn't scare people away but rather, they should foster belonging. At the end of the day, when we offer access to DEI, it becomes a building block for companies.

Let's take the first step in our journey by asking ourselves what DEI is and why it matters.

CHAPTER ONE

What is DEI?

Before we can dive into how to improve DEI, we have to define it. In short, DEI stands for diversity, equity, and inclusion — diversity is representation, equity is equal access to opportunities, and inclusion is creating a sense of belonging by ensuring that everyone feels welcomed and valued.

Just like anything that's widely discussed, there's a lot of misinformation out there — let's start by clearing up what DEI *isn't*.

What DEI Isn't

If you ask someone what DEI is, you'll probably get several different answers. Unfortunately, some of them might represent these initiatives and their purpose in a negative light. This, of course, isn't conducive to making change, so let's debunk some myths about DEI before we go any further.

1) It's not about "othering"

DEI isn't about shining a spotlight on any particular person or group that we perceive as different. We don't get to make the judgment that someone is different — we have to ask them how they perceive themselves and let them tell their own story instead of making assumptions.

2) It's not about shaming, blaming, or attacking anyone's character

No one should get shamed, blamed, or disinvited from the conversation. Often, when we talk about discrimination or "-isms," there's a person or group of people who might feel like they're at fault, especially if they're in a dominant group. They might feel as if they're causing these discriminatory situations, or feel like their character is being attacked.

It makes sense - at the very center of everyone's identity is their character. None of us want our character to be challenged or undermined, so naturally we might get defensive if we feel like our core is being attacked. So when we enter these conversations, we need to encourage self-awareness for everyone involved.

That especially includes white men, who might feel strongly that they're the target of these conversations as they're the dominant group in many corporate environments. We want to allow them to feel like they have a voice here because we absolutely need everyone's voice. And if white men are still dominating the workforce, it doesn't make sense to exclude them.

In fact, what makes more sense is to invite them in and allow them to feel like their voice is just as valuable as anyone else's. DEI discussions are an equalizer.

3) No one knows everything, and no one is free of biases

Even if someone is from a particular group, it doesn't mean that they know absolutely everything, or that they have all the answers about their issues. They also can't teach everybody everything. Everyone's experiences are unique, even if they share a common background.

It's also important to note that no one is free of biases. If the word bias bothers you, then replace it with preferences or habits. Let's not get so caught up in the word that we miss the larger message.

The misconception I often get is that if you are biased then you are prejudiced or racist. These two terms are mutually exclusive and do not mean the same thing. A bias has to do with preferences or familiarity towards people you feel comfortable with, and that level of comfort is rooted in stereotypes or single narratives. Those narratives derive from discrimination that the individual has subconsciously picked up.

This doesn't mean the person themselves is prejudiced, racist or xenophobic — they are often unaware that in their efforts to include certain people, they are actually excluding others.

For instance, someone might believe that a person who went to an Ivy League school is superior to someone who went to community college because everyone in their community growing up expressed that opinion, or because they saw the positive representation of the Ivy League in the media growing up. Or if someone grew up in a city, they might subconsciously view a candidate from a rural area as less educated or "cultured" without even realizing it.

We all have the opportunity to learn. Each of us have invaluable experiences that we should share to further understand each other and our own biases. It's an ongoing process — no one has completely mastered DEI or gotten rid of their biases. We have to keep evaluating and re-evaluating what we're doing and how we can continue to improve.

4) It's not just checking a box or having one representative from multiple groups

DEI isn't something we can cross off our to-do lists and put behind us, or something where we can hit our target or quota before moving on. Having two black people, one person from the Lesbian, Gay, Bisexual, Transgendered, Queer, Intersex, Asexual or Ally

(LGBTQIA+) community, and one woman might *look* like diversity, but diversity according to whom? At what point does being the only one in a group become more of a burden than anything, as we discussed above?

There are instances where quotas and targets are important, depending on the situation, organization, or team. However, if we're only focused on checking that off and we're not doing the work to reinforce what we've done, DEI becomes one dimensional and unscalable.

5) It doesn't reduce the quality of a company's work

Many people hear "increasing diversity" and fear that along with that comes hiring people because they check a box and not because they're qualified. This simply isn't the case. Doing so would lower productivity, which isn't anyone's goal, and the assumption that under-represented groups are inherently unqualified isn't true either.

Instead, increasing diversity means bringing in candidates who meet the requirements for the role, but also bringing a different perspective that can add value to your bottom line.

6) No one will be displaced

Another fear I've heard, particularly from white men, is that increasing diversity will cause them to lose their jobs. Again, this is a myth – smart companies find a way to leverage an increase in talent. Often, this means creating more jobs, and having more levels within a company for promotions. Having more qualified talent in the company is a good problem and it doesn't mean anyone is at risk of losing his/her/their job, unless there's an issue with performance.

7) It's not just for minorities or under-represented groups

The way that diversity, equity, and inclusion has been presented historically is that it's pursued to benefit minorities or other under-represented groups exclusively, as if they're the only ones impacted. And that mentality only leads to DEI being seen as an extracurricular activity, something that's a burden when taking the company's primary objectives into consideration.

Also, the reality is that many at the executive level are white men who might not feel as incentivized to tackle this work or make it a priority. This is especially true if it feels like something that's not valuable. It then becomes one of many projects that companies involve themselves with, lumped in with other noble causes that aren't at the top of the company's to-do list.

We need to reposition DEI as something that's directly valuable to the bottom line and to everyone in a company (something we'll discuss later in this chapter). Diversity goes way beyond skin color, gender, and sexual orientation.

So, What Is DEI, Anyway?

Now that we know what DEI *isn't* about, we can finally explore what it is. As we defined at the beginning, there's diversity, equity, and inclusion. In the past, it was excusable for companies to not take initiative around DEI, but with everything that's happened nationally with police brutality and other race-related incidents recently, those days are behind us.

It would be irresponsible for an organization to turn a blind eye to these issues. They're all throughout the media, other organizations are engaging in the discussion, and employees notice and care. It would be a disservice for organizations to ignore it.

Some companies focus on one, two, or all three of the elements of DEI at a time, in whatever order makes sense for their organization. Some put the equity piece first because they want to lay out the foundation and groundwork for compensation, and others might focus on creating an inclusive atmosphere before increasing diversity or tackling equity.

Historically, a lot of organizations have only focused on diversity, and that's why I believe that there's so much more work to be done, even with all the efforts these companies have made over the past couple of years. Diversity, equity, and inclusion are like a three-part harmony. They're stronger together and aren't as effective without the others.

There can be many members of minority groups in an organization, but people might feel unwelcome or like they're being excluded from certain initiatives. Or there could be diversity, but without equal access to programs or promotions that could help people grow in their careers. We need equity to sustain diversity and inclusion — we want DEI, not DIE.

Most importantly, DEI isn't a one-size-fits-all mentality. An organization's brand or mission is the filter through which DEI should be viewed. For example, say there's a car company and their mission is to make sure that everyone who drives their luxury vehicles is comfortable and safe when they drive. How does DEI trickle down from their big picture mission? That could look like giving everyone the access to try out their cars or feel connected to the brand, no matter who they are.

As hiring managers, you need to know what's happening overall on a holistic level in an organization, and whether your organization is sponsoring D, E, and I.

To get a clearer picture of what DEI really looks like, we'll have to dig a little deeper into what each individual piece really means.

Diversity

Many companies present diversity as something that's one dimensional, as if it's only about race, gender, and sexual orientation — the things we can see or quickly use to differentiate people from one another. That can make anyone who's not a part of a marginalized or under-represented group feel like they can't be a part of the conversation, undermining DEI efforts. Or on the other end of the spectrum, people can emphasize diversity of thought alone over everything else, which ignores how one's culture or physical attributes affect diversity of thought.

These two ends of the spectrum have to come together — people have to understand how diversity of thought is influenced by someone's culture, and how variances among people from different cultures are influenced by physical and biological attributes that vary from person to person. Some aspects of diversity should take priority over others, but at the end of the day, it's all connected.

In order to make everyone feel like they're a part of the conversation, we have to evolve our definition of "diversity" into something that's three layers versus one.

The first layer of diversity is internal — our physical and biological attributes like race, gender, ethnicity, ability (whether someone is physically, developmentally or mentally able), or age. In other words, the typical things people think of when they hear the word diversity.

The next layer is external, which is often cultural. This element is based on our environment and sometimes directly or indirectly linked to our physical and biological attributes. Some examples of this are socioeconomic status, marital status, nationality, language, religion, or what region we're from.

Just as external attributes can be connected to someone's physical appearance, the third layer of diversity connects with someone's cultural background. I consider this layer the business and experiential attributes of diversity, or diversity of thought. Things that fall under this category include communication, behavior, problem-solving, and leadership style.

Before we move on, I want to clarify that I'm not suggesting this third layer is some sort of Darwinian theory where people of certain backgrounds are prone to do a particular thing. But what I am suggesting is that when people have certain backgrounds, they're more susceptible to certain environmental or societal experiences, such as historical systemic inequities. These experiences can influence our behavior or personality.

Let's look at a hypothetical example — say there's an Asian woman working at a company based on the east coast. Her first layer would be the fact that she's Asian and a woman, where many diversity initiatives would stop.

Diving into her second layer, we could see that she's one of the few people on her team who grew up in the Midwest, adding a valuable perspective on customers or clients from that area.

On her third layer, she may be a natural extrovert in a team of introverts, or she might have gone to school in another country. There's much more to this woman's diversity than just her physical attributes.

This multi-layered approach to diversity ensures that everyone feels like they're a part of the conversation, especially people from more dominant groups who have never thought they added to the diversity of an organization.

Given the state of diversity at the executive level, this is incredibly important. Senior management is still overwhelmingly white and male, so they're often the ones who can start the first steps towards new DEI initiatives. These executives might not feel invited to these conversations, so it's important that we find a language that feels comfortable for everyone and opens the floor to all.

In instances like this, starting with the business and experiential side of diversity is probably the best approach. It's readily accessible to everyone and more digestible for people who might be tip-toeing around the conversation. From there, the dialogue can grow to encompass the other layers of diversity.

No one is exempt from this work, not even people in non-dominant groups. By openly acknowledging our differences and constructing our conversations in a way that makes everyone feel comfortable speaking, we can begin to see where we're similar despite our differences and connect everyone on a new level.

Equity

Like diversity, equity is often taken out of context and pressed into a one-dimensional space. People hear it and get uncomfortable, immediately thinking, "Oh boy, this is about compensation." Certainly, making sure there's compensation equity across race, ethnicity, and gender is a component of it.

But more specifically, equity is made up of three parts — distribution, fairness, and access.

Distribution of money, awards, and recognition isn't what people think about when it comes to equity. Is there distribution across different teams and different people? Or do the same people get recognition or projects or promotions every time?

Fairness is fairly straightforward. Are we being fair in our processes and practices? One example I like to share is about a team I was on at a company. I was on the same level as two of my other colleagues, though I had a different position. We all started at the company weeks apart and, shortly thereafter, the company moved locations. There were only three offices that were available to the team — one went to our boss, and the other two went to my colleagues.

My boss said that my efforts were driving the success of the entire team, but if that was the case, why was I not given one of the offices? Maybe there was a reason as to why I didn't get an office that my colleagues did. That's something I'll always wonder about. I never brought it up because I was afraid I would come across as petty. But in an instance like this, the question would be, well, how were the office assignments determined?

But when we think about fairness and truly being equitable, we get to revisit these kinds of examples. How do we create equity and fairness in assigning something as simple as an office space? That's the kind of mindset we want to be in as managers — to challenge ourselves by re-evaluating the decisions we've made in the last six months to a year and asking, "How can I justify my decision as being equitable?"

Access to opportunities is one of the biggest factors in equity. Think about all the opportunities that are offered in an organization — mentorship programs, chats with senior leadership, initiatives, or even physical proximity to a company's headquarters. Is everyone in your company able to access these things? In cases like physical proximity to the company headquarters, is there a way that employees can easily bridge that gap?

Access leads to opportunities, so if everyone in an organization doesn't have the same access, they won't get the chance to progress like someone who has that access.

On a broader scale, access can mean broadening the network of candidates. This doesn't mean we have to have a quota, or that we have to pick out one person from a single demographic. It just means that we ask ourselves if we've been giving people from various backgrounds across all three layers of diversity the opportunity to apply to be in our organization. Taking this approach to widen the pool of qualified candidates is known as diverse slate hiring[1].

For instance, if you run an internship program, have you opened it up to a variety of schools, or do you reach out to the same ones year after year? Are you making sure that a range of potential interns know that these opportunities exist and that if they get the position, they'll have access to everything they need to excel?

I also want to note that equity isn't the same thing as equality. Equality is about everyone getting the exact same thing. Equity is about finding the fairest way to provide people with what they need to achieve their goals and objectives.

A commonly-taught example of equity involves three people looking over a fence — one person is 6'7", another is 5'10", and the last is 5'6". The tallest person doesn't have any problems seeing over the fence, so he doesn't need a boost. The person who is 5'10"

---

[1] https://lattice.com/library/does-diverse-slate-hiring-work

can see a little bit, but with a small step, they can see over. The final person gets the biggest boost since they have the farthest to go to see over the fence.

If they were going for equality, everyone would have gotten the middle step, which wouldn't help the shortest person see over the fence at all and would have been redundant for the tallest person.

Another example I like to give is being a fifth-grade teacher. They're teaching the same curriculum to all the students, but the students all have different backgrounds and needs. One might have dyslexia, another might have access to tutors at home, and another might be left alone a lot because their parents work late.

It wouldn't be realistic to expect all of the students to need the same support from their teacher to achieve the same grades. However, the teacher would want to make sure that each student had the adequate support and resources to potentially reach the same outcome. Some of us might feel like it's not fair for one child to get special treatment over another. This is where we get to be honest with ourselves and admit that the child with a tutor already has a boost. It's true that he shouldn't be penalized because his parents can afford a tutor, but the child whose parents work late, or the dyslexic child, shouldn't be penalized either.

Essentially, equity is meeting people where they are based on their needs, but I want to emphasize that equity doesn't mean that expectations are different for different people. We always want to bring in qualified candidates who can do the job, but we have to consider that everyone has different experiences, and therefore might need different feedback or guidance to get to the goals that you set for them.

Inclusion

Inclusion is key to sustaining DEI efforts. Even if you ensure that everyone has equal access to opportunities or that there's a diverse group of people on your team, no one will stay if they feel alienated or excluded. Inclusion is about welcoming people and making sure that they know they're a valued member of the team. It means that everyone gets the sense that they belong.

In the introduction, I shared my experience of being a middle manager with years of experience under my belt and being terrified to go to work every day. I didn't feel welcomed. I didn't feel included.

And there are little nuances that prevent people from feeling included. An obvious one is when someone feels that they are the only person who looks or thinks like them within their team, or even their whole company. That can lead to tokenism, which puts pressure on someone to represent their entire group, upholding or being the exception to a stereotype, affecting work performance. We'll talk about tokenism in more detail in chapter seven.

On the flip side, we might have someone who offers a diverse perspective or representation within a seemingly diverse group, but they don't feel safe or comfortable. They might overcompensate or under compensate in their performance or personality in response.

For anyone who doesn't understand how isolating being the only person within your demographic or with your perspective can feel, I want to challenge you to flip the script. Imagine you're the only person who was your race, gender, or ethnicity, and when you walk into work, no one acknowledges you, or everyone notices you because you're different.

You might feel unique for the first couple of days, but if you've spent the majority of your life being the only one, going from work to home and back without seeing anyone like you, you could feel isolated or even a little unwelcome.

Inclusion also involves the idea of integration. Mergers and acquisitions are a prime example of how companies can create inclusion. During a merger or acquisition, companies have to bring everyone together, rally them under one idea, belief, and company. And the same process one would use to do that is the same action that would be used for any type of inclusion efforts. It's making people feel welcomed, making everyone feel like they're part of one team.

One of the best and most effective ways to start making people feel welcome is acknowledging how each person is unique and different first. The notion of forcing people to see themselves as a unit before we celebrate our differences backfires, especially in the context of race. The Colorblind Theory is an example of this; it suggests that we shouldn't see color, which can feel like an omission of a person's experience if they are Black, Indigenous or Persons of Color (BIPOC). Once you celebrate everyone's differences and understand the value they bring, you can work towards one common belief or pledge to become united.

Pushing the "you have to follow our way or else" mentality doesn't really make anyone feel valued, so it behooves us to learn to hear from other people and let the room fill with unique voices.

The problem is that many companies tend to avoid the discussions that can bring these unique voices forward. But why? And in what ways are these discussions important for an organization as a whole?

Why We Avoid DEI Discussions

1) We position it as a cause, not a priority

As we discussed at the beginning of the chapter, sometimes DEI is lumped in with charitable causes instead of being considered a necessary part of a business's bottom line. It can feel like an obligation. We might throw money at it, or say nice words, then move on without actually changing anything. If it's not framed as something that can improve the company's profitability, it's more likely to get pushed to the back burner.

2) We don't give people permission to tie it to money or return on investment

Giving people equal representation across different groups, ensuring there's equity, and making everyone feel included is great, of course, but let's also acknowledge that it drives business, money, and market share. People who connect finances with DEI are often called exploitative, but that's not the case. DEI is deeply linked with profitability and productivity, as we'll soon explore.

The sooner we can acknowledge that fact, the sooner we can give everybody permission to connect DEI and profitability. In doing so, we can pull in more dominant groups who might not yet see it as a priority. Once they understand that diversity goes beyond skin color, gender, or sexual orientation and can improve the bottom line, then DEI can become a part of our everyday experience and culture.

3) We only make it about race, gender, sexual orientation, or ethnicity

Right now, many people hear DEI and they only think of those four categories. It *is* about those things, but as you know by now, there's so much more to it. If we reduce it to those categories, then anyone who doesn't belong to an under-represented group might not feel like they can join in or might not be incentivized to help.

There's also a level of guilt there, whether it's actively recognized or subliminally suggested, that can make people resistant to diving into DEI. These four categories are critical and hold the highest priority, especially in the US where there's a long history of discrimination in those groups, but people might not be ready to tackle such big topics right away.

The best way to massage the conversation is to remind people that there are different ways to see diversity.

4) We're conditioned to not acknowledge differences

Even though we all see differences, we're told that we shouldn't actually acknowledge or vocalize that we see them. So we walk around, seeing that people are different — that someone is a man or a woman or a certain shade of brown — but we say nothing because if we do, we might be seen as discriminatory.

But in effect, we're not able to bring to light the stories, stereotypes, and biases we carry because we're trying to negate them instead. And that means nothing actually changes.

5) We don't give people permission to ask questions or make mistakes

Conversations around DEI can seem extremely intimidating because of all the jargon that we hear. These terms sound so brilliant in an academic context, but they don't transfer well to the workplace. We get caught up in saying phrases without getting a deeper understanding of them, and we spend less time saying what we actually mean.

As I touched on in the introduction, this jargon can become daunting for people, and people are often afraid to ask questions about it in fear that they'll say the wrong thing. They don't want to be labeled as ignorant, racist or politically incorrect, so they don't say anything at all. Because people can often get so defensive in DEI conversations, or fall into a mode of trying to prove a point, they might not necessarily give someone the space to make a mistake.

No one wants to be attacked, so they stay quiet, but when people stay quiet, nothing changes. We need to take a step back and enter these discussions without getting defensive, fearful of saying the wrong thing, or being hypercritical of everything someone says. We'll talk more about how to do this in chapter five. Everyone has the opportunity to learn because no one is free from biases.

6) There's the assumption that there's only one right way to talk about it

Some people who are driving DEI efforts suggest or assume that there's only one right way to talk about the subject — their way.

That becomes a very exclusionary way of thinking, which undermines the whole idea of diversity, equity, and inclusion. If that's the approach we take in an organization, then that becomes a different problem because we're just perpetuating our own ideas. A person might not agree and not fully understand or commit to DEI efforts.

Instead, we have to listen and understand other approaches. It doesn't mean that we have to agree, it just means that we get to use that space to listen, expand our minds, and create heightened awareness.

7) There's pressure to fix things fast

Companies are facing a lot of pressure to be more inclusive, diverse, and equitable, which makes some feel like they have to fix their company as quickly as possible. That's a lot of pressure put on everyone to get it done instead of getting it right. It's just a reaction, not a commitment to change.

And it's also insulting to both the people who have been doing this work for a long time and to the under-represented groups who have been dealing with systematic oppression for centuries or decades; it suggests that they couldn't figure it out, but someone in another group could change their entire organization in a matter of days.

This isn't like putting tape over a hole in the wall and expecting it to be permanently fixed. Reacting quickly to something just to avoid a long, difficult conversation will ultimately hurt in the long run.

8) We feel uncomfortable

Expanding on my previous point, DEI conversations can be really uncomfortable and no one likes to feel that way. But let me ask you this — when was the last time any of us felt 100% comfortable in our jobs or careers? The whole point of growth is feeling discomfort, and through that discomfort, we grow. My motto is to stay safe but push the boundaries of what comfort means to you.

9) It feels like a lot of work

In large, global companies, there are so many layers to everything that DEI just feels like a lot of work. Since DEI isn't often presented as a business imperative, but as a side project, it feels burdensome. I have often seen DEI get dumped on someone's lap who doesn't have a background in this work. While DEI isn't exclusive to just experts, strategies should be spearheaded by an expert.

In many instances where there is an expert, they are single-handedly expected to magically fix all DEI-related issues in an organization. It's no wonder that the average tenure for a Chief Diversity Officer is 3.2 years[2]. All too often, companies think tackling DEI means running a bunch of programs. Without having a clear strategy and a process, the programs start to feel burdensome when they are scaled.

There are also several nuances based not only on regions, but globally. In some countries, class structures are stricter and racial categories are different.

Under-represented individuals might internalize these structures and not see anything wrong with them. The dominant group might not either, so trying to tackle DEI in a situation where many might not see a problem in the first place is daunting.

Gather people's experiences, thoughts, and concerns from all levels of the company, then develop a DEI strategy and mission statement based on their feedback. Once those are locked in, you can figure out how to execute the initiatives in all of your regions and offices.

10) It's personal to us

Diversity, equity, and inclusion are so personal to us. We've either been the subject of discrimination, or been accused of being biased. And it brings up emotions that we have carried with us for a long time. We don't want to bring those feelings back up again or end up in a similar situation, so we refrain from talking about it.

But then, we don't hear each other's stories and celebrate how we're unique. DEI efforts can help us identify parallels between each other, and that's where the unification really begins.

---

[2] https://www.bloomberg.com/opinion/articles/2021-01-18/don-t-let-chief-diversity-officer-be-a-dead-end-job

The Tangible Benefits of DEI

Despite all the reasons we might be hesitant to jump into DEI, the journey is well worth it. Yes, there's the emotional and mental component of making sure that everyone feels safe, represented, and included at work. But as I touched on in the reasons why we avoid DEI conversations, investing time and energy into DEI initiatives is great for the bottom line. We can see the benefits in three major ways:

1) It increases ROI and productivity

DEI initiatives are about people, and putting effort in to create a diverse, inclusive space makes a noticeable difference in productivity and retention. As we've discussed in this chapter, feeling valued goes a long way in helping someone produce their best work. Instead of dealing with the distractions that come along with feeling isolated, they can focus entirely on their work.

This increase in productivity goes a long way in increasing a company's ROI. A McKinsey study showed that effective DEI results in 33% improved profitability[3]. That's a significant jump. On the flip side, turnover attributed to unfairness and bias results in a $64 billion annual loss for companies across the US, according to a Korn/Ferry study[4]. Rapid turnover decreases morale, increases costs, and lowers productivity — all things that hurt the bottom line.

Companies with more diversity are more innovative, resilient, and better equipped to respond to complex problems as well. In a

---

[3] https://www.mckinsey.com/~/media/mckinsey/business%20functions/organization/our%20insights/delivering%20through%20diversity/delivering-through-diversity_full-report.ashx

[4] https://www.kornferry.com/content/dam/kornferry/docs/article-migration/The%20Corporate%20Leavers%20Survey%20.pdf

constantly changing world, this is a skill that will give companies that invested in DEI a long-term advantage.

2) It appeals to conscious consumers and employees

Consumers are getting much smarter and they want to buy and do business with organizations that are socially responsible. Doing things like partnering with an organization that works for a cause they care about, making an effort to increase representation in your employee base, or having marketing that resonates across multiple demographics, you can connect with more customers.

If a consumer has to choose between two companies selling the same product, they'll likely pick the one that aligns with their values the most; 63% of consumers prefer to buy from a brand that reflects their own values[5]. By investing in DEI, we're essentially increasing market share, demand and interest.

Now more than ever, employees also look to how a company responds to external diversity-related issues. Do they put up a superficial hashtag and call it a day? Or are they really committing to putting in authentic work to back up whatever's said on social media? Are they consistent and deliberate in when and how they respond?

Increasingly, people want to work for organizations that are putting in the work to include them, which improves retention and referral rates. Both of these things have a direct impact to the bottom line, saving money on onboarding new employees and bringing in more high-quality talent.

---

[5] https://newsroom.accenture.com/news/majority-of-consumers-buying-from-companies-that-take-a-stand-on-issues-they-care-about-and-ditching-those-that-dont-accenture-study-finds.htm

3) It prepares a workforce for the future

According to the Bureau of Labor Statistics, the majority of the workforce will be people of color by 2032 so, not only will the workforce look visibly different, but there will be even more variance within the other layers of diversity that will need to be addressed. This means that the dynamics within companies will change drastically, and if we're not changing with the times, we're doing our teams a disservice.

By starting now, we give our companies time to get comfortable with DEI and learn how to navigate it in the workplace. They won't have to stop to pivot or adjust to change — their productivity will remain high even in the face of change.

How Do We Address DEI Now Rather Than Later?

Reading all of this has hopefully made it clear that DEI isn't going away, and it needs to be tackled sooner rather than later. Plus, it's just the human thing to do, and it's an admirable journey to embark on.

However as we discussed above, there are already corporate initiatives and hashtags that are trying to make up the gap, but we don't see significant progress.

That's because we aren't tapping into the most powerful resource a company has: its middle management.

Exercises

Your Turn:

Directions: Walk through the list of diversity attributes listed in column 1 and 2 below. Answer the following questions:

1. What is the dominant group for each diversity attribute listed in column 1 and 2?
2. How might being part of the dominant group within each of the diversity attributes impact your work style (behavior, communication, leadership, management, and personality) listed in column 3?
3. How might being part of an under-represented group within each category impact your work style (behavior, communication, leadership, management, and personality) listed in column 3?

Example: As far as race goes, the dominant group is white. Being white in the workplace might impact behavior because I might feel more comfortable and confident in the workplace and on my team being more people who resemble me. If I'm a Black, Indigenous and/or Person of Color (BIPOC) which is part of an under-represented group, I may not be as outgoing in my job because I fear scrutiny because I look different.

Table 1

Column 1	Column 2	Column 3
Level 1: Physical/Biological	Level 1: Physical/Biological	Level 3: Business/Work Style
• Age • Sexual Orientation • Race • Ethnicity • Ableism/Physical Functioning • Gender Identity • Color	• Age • Sexual Orientation • Race • Ethnicity • Ableism/Physical Functioning • Gender Identity • Color	• Behavior Style • Communication Style • Leadership Style • Management Style

Take it to Your Team:

During your next team meeting, set aside 30 minutes for this exercise. Ask people on your team to do the following and answer the questions below. Be sure to be the first person to kick it off (you should answer questions as it relates specifically to race). The goal of this discussion is to gain awareness on how your team can be more diverse and make sure everyone is clear on the value it will bring to the overall business:

1. Select one category from the various diversity attributes.
2. How might increasing diversity in that category on our team benefit us in the following ways:
   a. Working with cross functional partners?
   b. Problem solving within our team?
   c. How might it benefit the product or service that our company offers and our contribution to it?

CHAPTER TWO

Why Middle Management is Key to DEI Success

The power of middle management first dawned on me at my first job, straight out of grad school as a budget analyst. I didn't have much background in budgeting except for the graduate courses that I took in the subject, but I needed to sustain myself and I wanted to learn how to enjoy it (or at least how to be good at it). The only way I could do that is if I was under somebody's tutelage who I really respected and admired. That was exactly who I found.

A man who I'll call Victor was the head of the department, and in my interview he said, "You know, Martine, you have great energy and you're clearly a smart person. I think you're capable of doing the job. But how do I know you would commit to this job when you haven't done any type of work related to budgeting in your internships?"

I really respected him for being so direct and honest in asking this question. He was the kind of person I wanted to work for, someone who could figure me out, challenge me, and help me grow. He hadn't said what he said to intimidate me; he was just getting me to think more deeply about what I wanted.

That's at the heart of managing somebody — challenging someone and driving them in the middle of that challenge.

Four months after I started, Victor put in his resignation. I was devastated. Just the very act of him leaving so soon was nothing short of ironic and made me want to leave.

My new manager was much more of a micro-manager, the kind of boss who wanted everybody to be a carbon copy of her. Even though she would say things like, "You're allowed to ask silly or dumb questions," she would always react by making a face or sort of mocking the person who asked.

It inhibited my growth in a lot of ways, and her lack of patience made me a little bit insecure and nervous. I didn't want to tackle a new challenge or approach her with questions. I was put off from doing everything that would push me to evolve and progress in my career.

My point is, managers can really influence a person's career trajectory and the way they see life. If a manager isn't aware of their behavior or biases, they can drastically affect someone's experience and a company's DEI efforts, especially since they have influence and involvement at every level of a company.

They hire new employees, push for their promotions, liaise with senior executives, and affect who decides to stay or leave. Unlike the executive suite, they're interacting with employees at various levels and can directly take part in bringing in more diverse employees or carrying out a company's DEI vision.

Creating change from the top just doesn't work. Senior management doesn't have the bandwidth to see any initiatives through, nor does Human Resources (HR). In order to understand middle management's influence across all areas of a company even further, and how it can lead to progress or can hinder DEI initiatives, we need to talk about implicit bias.

Implicit Bias

All the ways that middle management can affect DEI success start with implicit bias – the beliefs we have about certain groups that we aren't entirely conscious of. These preferences are influenced by the environment we grew up in, what we see as the traditional, dominant culture and what the media portrays as preferable or ideal.

All of these ideas get so embedded and ingrained in our subconscious that we don't even realize that these beliefs can lead us to unintentionally exclude a particular group. Say someone grew up in the US, consuming popular movies and TV shows. Many pieces of media, particularly right after 9/11, portrayed Muslim people in a negative light. If someone didn't acknowledge that they had that uninformed bias, they might pass over a qualified Muslim person or an individual whom they perceive to be Muslim in a candidate pool.

When we think about DEI initiatives, we need to start by acknowledging that we all have implicit bias, regardless of who we are. Everyone has past experiences and has internalized messages from the people around them, whether they notice that or not. By acknowledging our individual biases, we can begin to learn how to mitigate them, and in doing so, we can make our management decisions as fair as possible.

Since managers have such a tremendous impact on every area of a company, addressing implicit bias can make a massive change within an organization. Let's break down how managers can impact diversity, equity, and inclusion in every part of the people management process.

Middle Management and Diversity

A middle manager's impact on diversity starts before an employee even gets hired and continues throughout an employee's time at a company.

Recruiting

Recruiting efforts don't have to be about quotas, which historically have been seen as "checking a box" or, as we talked about in chapter one, "bringing down" the quality of employees in an organization. This is where some people get stuck. They fear that they will be forced into diversity, which can turn away people who sense that the efforts aren't coming from an authentic place.

I suggest we cast a wider net by sourcing more candidates. A Harvard study shows that if you increase the number of candidates from under-represented groups in your search for a candidate, then you increase your chances of hiring a qualified candidate from an under-represented group[6].

Let's imagine a female-majority company. If there's one man applying for a job among six women, then the likelihood of the man getting the position is low. As the number of male applicants grows, let's say to three, then the chances of a man being hired for the role increases.

Hiring managers have the power to change this. They influence who gets recruited, working directly with recruiters or HR to write the job description and identify what kind of individuals they'd like to fill a job opening. They can provide their preferences, which they should evaluate for any implicit biases, and ask themselves, "What looks the same? How are these candidates the same or different? Can we search in other environments? Is anyone being excluded?"

Also carefully consider the job description and how candidates from different backgrounds might interpret the job qualifications.

---

[6] https://hbr.org/2016/04/if-theres-only-one-woman-in-your-candidate-pool-theres-statistically-no-chance-shell-be-hired

For instance, studies show that certain groups, such as white men, are more likely to apply for positions that are slightly outside of their comfort level, or where they don't meet every job qualification[7]. Generally speaking, they are more conditioned to seeing it as a stretch assignment and will apply for the position anyway.

However, another group might take the job description literally and feel that they have to meet every criteria of the job description in order to apply for it. In this case, something as basic as a job description might deter an entire pool of candidates from taking interest in your organization.

This is the reason actively looking for candidates is invaluable. Ask for referrals from diverse pools of employees, or start asking for references from inside your company to diversify your candidate pool.

Essentially, managers are filtering what recruiters are looking for. Sometimes, hiring managers might not know where else to look, but proactively asking a recruiter about where they haven't looked yet, or if there are any organizations or backgrounds that they haven't explored can make a huge difference in bringing in more diverse candidates.

Asking for referrals from diverse pools of employees is another way that managers can diversify the recruitment process. Instead of always going outside to start gathering a pool of candidates, try asking for help from inside.

---

[7] https://abcnews.go.com/Business/women-aggressive-men-applying-jobs-hired-frequently-linkedin/story?id=61531741

The hiring process

Throughout the hiring process, a manager gets even more involved in creating a diverse team. They can ask themselves, "Am I being consistent in asking every candidate the same questions, and am I being equitable at all stages?" Some people have challenged me and said, "Martine, asking every candidate the same questions in the same order feels very static. Interviews are about getting to know the individual."

And that's true. But what I would say is that those initial questions should absolutely be consistent across the board. Sometimes, our first impressions are based on how we interpret a candidate's resumé or that first face-to-face interaction, which are influenced by our biases. In asking everyone the same questions, at least at the start of an interview, we level the playing field and mitigate biases. After that, you can freestyle the conversation more and tailor the follow-up questions.

Also try to be consistent in how you format your interviews across all candidates. If you meet with one candidate in person in a conference room, try to do the same with all candidates. This might seem obvious, but as workplaces become increasingly virtual, it's important to keep this in mind.

Something as simple as someone's name can suggest what a person looks like. For example, if we see a resumé and the person's name is LaShonda, subconsciously we know that this person is most likely African-American. Knowing that triggers certain beliefs and certain sentiments about that person. If we see that LaShonda went to Harvard, that triggers other beliefs.

As humans, we might feel bothered or concerned about whether LaShonda is a good candidate before even meeting her due to stereotypes associated with African-Americans. Some companies mitigate these implicit biases by omitting anything that suggests someone's background, but not all organizations do or should, depending on their field.

Before meeting with someone, identify and dissect why you might have a feeling about them based on their resumé — is it bias? What's driving you to feel that way? How can you remove that bias from your decision-making?

When reviewing applicants, a clear indication of bias is when you have "a good feeling" about a candidate, or you notice something about them that seems familiar. Instead, focus on the job qualifications and continue to ask yourself, "Can this person do the job?" If you get caught up with someone's behavior, such as the fact that they are so pleasant or have a nice voice, ask yourself, "How does this tie back to his/her/their ability to do the job?"

Biases are formed by habits. To unlock our hiring biases, we should consider enhancing our current habits around hiring. Making fair hiring decisions requires a lot of self-awareness.

Representation

Since hiring managers are the ones who are filtering who gets recruited and choosing who gets hired, they're influencing the actual representation and demographics within their teams. As we discussed in chapter one, representation doesn't necessarily mean filling quotas or checking off boxes, but they can be a great initial step to understanding the value of diversity.

In understanding the value of representation and the impact it can have on a team's growth and success, hiring managers can continue to evaluate whether their teams are truly diverse and do the work that's necessary to be an active ally every day – more on what being an active ally means later in chapter five.

Middle Management and Equity

Middle management's role in equity can go a long way in leveling the playing field within a company, and by extension, an industry as a whole. As I mentioned in chapter one, the first thing that people think of when they hear equity is compensation, so let's start there.

Compensation

Managers influence the compensation of each employee because they also put in budget requests that could give their team higher salaries or change the salary distribution. They can challenge HR if they feel like the compensation is not equitable enough across different people on their team, or ask HR to partner with them in conducting a compensation analysis during performance reviews.

This can be a great opportunity to create equity, not just in the gender pay gap, but in race and other diversity dimensions as well. We can also look at pay equity at various intersections of categories, like race and gender, or age and sexual orientation and see whether things are unbalanced. They can even look into salary bands by teams, departments or positions. Managers have the power to drive these discussions with HR — something that HR likely won't initiate due to bandwidth constraints — and create equity that's tailored to the unique diversity of their team.

As those individuals are promoted, that equity follows them, which facilitates equity not just on the team, but across the organization.

Career mobility and promotions

Managers are responsible for deciding who gets promoted and grows within an organization, creating pipelines for who gets to move forward. Naturally, this is a powerful spot to be in. Managers can create strategies and processes for supporting and promoting people that take equity into account.

Managers should look at what factors affect someone's performance, and by extension, what can help them move forward. Where are we not supporting people enough for them to move forward? How might a person's background affect their productivity and confidence? What might be causing a gap in performance? Do we have biases that are being overlooked, which lead to some people being left behind? How can we be equitable in supporting individuals as they move up in a company?

Managers can also run analyses to look at who they've promoted in the past — what are their demographics? Is there some sort of disparity? If there is, we can start to have more awareness of our biases. And that's not to shame or blame us. Instead, it gives us a benchmark and a target, plus an opportunity to change.

If there's a lack of change in promotions as they relate to DEI, companies will lose good people and lower morale. As with compensation, equity in career mobility spreads with an individual moving up the ladder and across an organization as a whole.

Middle Management and Inclusion

Like my story at the beginning of the chapter shows, managers can play a huge role in making someone feel like they belong at a company, something that strongly correlates with whether someone decides to stay or leave a job, as well as how much effort they put into their work.

Attrition and retention

Attrition is when people voluntarily leave an organization, and like I mentioned in chapter one, 38% of turnover is due to unfairness or bias. People might feel overlooked for promotions or opportunities, under-represented, or underpaid.

Someone is more likely to leave than stay and fight for what they feel they deserve if a manager is unaware of their unconscious biases and how they're affecting their team. They might feel that they're never going to win since bias isn't quantifiable — and they're left to their own assumptions as to why they're being overlooked assuming that their performance is good, and usually those assumptions have to do with how they are different.

I can't tell you how many times I've heard individuals from various organizations say, "You know, I was overlooked for an opportunity three or four times, but the person next to me got it. I got good feedback in my performance reviews. I still don't understand why I was overlooked because nothing was ever explained to me." That feeling can really alienate someone and push them to leave.

If a manager commits to DEI, they can push the attrition rate down. But if attrition stays up, managers should encourage HR to run metrics or have third parties facilitate exit interviews to understand why someone left and what their concerns were. Most likely, a person leaving won't share why they're leaving with their manager or HR in fear of retaliation, so ensuring anonymity can yield much better results.

Either way, it would behoove a manager to understand why people are leaving and look at the demographics of who's leaving. How quickly are they leaving? What roles are they leaving from? Understanding the patterns of promotion, compensation, and representation can help to slow attrition rates.

In reducing turnover, companies can maintain productivity and save on onboarding costs. And with the demographics of the workplace shifting to be mostly people of color, understanding how and why people might leave is key to the bottom line.

Retention results in the employee growing in experience. Experience is harder to quantify, but it's extremely important nonetheless. As I've mentioned, managers can motivate someone to do their best work, or make them not want to come to work at all. It's imperative that managers understand their own implicit biases and do the work for DEI in order to make all of their team feel valued.

How Can I Help?

Managers can bring much change to an organization, whether for good or bad. Seeing just how much power you have, you might be wondering how to actually make those changes beyond some of the examples we touched on. Let's start with the first step — understanding your personal benefits.

Your Turn:

Imagine that I've just invited you to help me in the interview process for a Marketing Director for a retail company. Your responsibility is to take 3 minutes and read over the candidate profiles. These are made-up profiles and not resumés because I want you to assume that both candidates are equally qualified for the position. What distinguishes them are the details in their profiles (below). Answer the series of questions below:

1. What inferences have you made about each candidate based on their profiles? In other words, describe the person based on their job profile.
2. Identify which of the two candidates you prefer based solely on the information provided. What's your rationale?

3. Consider the following:
   a. Is there a problem with hiring someone based on preferences that are not tied to their work experience?
   b. If so, how might hiring someone based on preference negatively affect your team and the business?
   c. What can we do to mitigate our potential biases during the interview process?
   d. Would you have any concerns if all of the candidates had resumés identical to William Jackson's or to Kenneth Bowie's?
   e. What can we do to ensure that all of the candidates that we are sourcing don't have identical profiles (e.g., all of the resumés are identical to William Jackson's or to Kenneth Bowie's)?

William Jackson
2818 Malcolm X Blvd.
New York, NY
Phone+1 (347) 441 7577

EXPERIENCE

DIRECTOR of Global MarkEting   New York, NY
Foot Locker
01/2016 – current

MARKETING DIRector   Philadelphia, PA
Five below
12/2012 – 11/2015

Senior director, Marketing   Philadelphia, PA
Burlington STORES
09/2003– 06/2012

Marketing Manager   NEW YORK, NY
Macy's Inc.
11/1997– 06/20o3

EDUCATION

UNIVERSITY OF THE DISTRICT OF COLUMBIA
Bachelor's Degree in Management, 1997

HOBBIES
Member, Bala Golf Club

Volunteer
Habitat for Humanity: 2006-present

Kenneth Bowie

395 Center Avenue
Fresno, CA 93704
Phone+1 (545) 576 7577

EXPERIENCE

DIRECTOR of Global marketing   LOS ANGELES, CA
LUXOTTICA Group
01/2016 – current

DIRECTOR of Global marketing   DALLAS, TX
Neiman Marcus
10/2012 – 11/2015

CORPORATE Marketing Director   ORLANDO, FL
AMerican retail group
07/2007 – 09/2012

Marketing Manager   ORLANDO, FL
AMerican retail group
09/2002– 06/2007

EDUCATION

Brown UNIVERSITY   PROVIDENCE, RI
Bachelor's Degree in Management, 2002

GREEK
Sigma Chi Fraternity

HOBBIES
Team Sports, Intramural Soccer
Ironman Triathlon

Take it to Your Team:

The next time that you interview to fill a position, consider doing the following:

1. Reach out to your Employee Resource Groups (ERGs) and/or Diversity Council and ask them if they have referrals.

2. Look at the list of resumés and ask yourself, "How are all of these candidates similar?"

3. Ask Recruiting/Talent Acquisition to provide you with a few more candidates who are dissimilar from your first set.

4. Be aware of your preferences that can cause you to be biased towards a candidate. Focus on each candidate's ability to meet the needs of the job description.

5. Ask each candidate the same set of initial questions in the same order before you freestyle the remainder of the interview.

CHAPTER THREE

Understanding Your Personal Privilege

We ended the last chapter with the phrase "personal benefits," but in the context of DEI, you've probably heard it called "privilege."

Being called "privileged" often stirs up feelings that runs through the core of who you are as a person. You might feel like someone is saying that you didn't work hard for anything, or that you don't deserve anything you've achieved. It almost implies that you're weaker than they are, or that anything you've been through wasn't bad because of some characteristic you have and likely can't change.

Basically, being called privileged can feel like an attack on your character.

What's missing from this definition of privilege is the context of where it came from. Certain terms that come from academia, like this one, aren't neatly translated into mainstream American lingo — people in academia might not necessarily appreciate the nuances in the corporate world and vice versa.

The word is packed with so much history, and the average person either doesn't know, understand, or have the time to learn about it. And because of this, being labeled as privileged feels like a baseless attack.

But we shouldn't get so caught up in the word that we lose its meaning: privilege is when you're innately given a benefit, advantage, or access to something that not everyone has.

I encourage anyone who doesn't like the word "privilege" to use a different one since the term is so triggering. When I lead sessions on the topic, people call it benefits, advantages, blessings, or luck. Whatever makes sense for you.

Let's unpack the nuances of the concept and see why "checking our privilege" is key to effective DEI.

What Privilege Isn't

As I mentioned above, privilege is a loaded term. It makes people feel like they're being attacked, or that others are making assumptions about them so, let's look into what privilege isn't before we discuss what it is.

1) It doesn't mean you didn't work hard or that you're undeserving

Privilege doesn't erase the fact that you have to work to achieve things and deserve your achievements. For instance, if you're a man who's in a higher-up position in a company, you didn't get there solely because of your gender. You worked hard and deserved to be recognized for that work. Your privilege just means that being chosen for that role wasn't entirely merit-based in that you had more access to certain spaces that helped you succeed.

2) It doesn't erase pain or struggle

Part of the reason why people feel attacked when others say they're privileged is because other people may not know what it took for them to get to where they are today. Let's use the example of a white man who grew up in an impoverished area in an emotionally abusive home and only has his high school diploma, where a majority of his counterparts have an advanced degree.

Someone might say he's privileged because he's white, but that's only the case in certain environments and contexts (which we'll get into shortly). Being white doesn't take away from the fact that he faced real economic hardships or that he never pursued higher education. It just means that he has an edge in situations where race plays into whether someone benefits or gets access to something.

3) It's not something to feel guilty about

When people realize that they have privilege, they might feel guilty about it. No one wants to feel like they're benefitting while others aren't, or that they owe people who may not have the same advantages.

Being privileged is not about feeling guilty, shamed, or blamed. It's about acknowledging the power we have, considering that not everyone has power in that area, and doing our best to support those people.

Privilege is something you need to recognize and use to mitigate your biases, and as you'll see, everyone has privilege. Yes, everyone, although our culture's understanding of the term tends to limit it to white people or men. But if our culture's definition isn't accurate, what does privilege really mean?

What is Privilege?

As I mentioned before, being privileged means that you receive benefits, advantages, or access to something based on whatever facets of diversity you happen to have, whether it's gender, race, sexual orientation, ableness or any of the other areas we touched on in previous chapters. It doesn't require you to think too much about it — you just have it while others don't. It's so innate that sometimes we don't even realize we have it.

Another way to think about it is that the privileged group is considered the "norm" in whatever context you're in. Ableness is a great example of this. When you're able-bodied, you're in the dominant group and you likely won't even think about whether doors are wide enough for a wheelchair or whether a manager will understand a depressive episode. But if you're physically, mentally, or developmentally disabled, these are things you have to consider in your day-to-day life just to exist.

In addition to these more evident elements of privilege, there are a few nuances that the traditional definition tends to miss:

1) Privilege can look different from one environment to another

In one place, you could have privilege, but in another, you might not, like in the example of the lower-income white man I used above. Using age as an example, being older at a long-standing insurance company could give you certain advantages, while being older at a tech start-up likely won't give you an edge.

2) Privilege can be the result of several things

Privilege is sometimes just the result of how things have always been historically. Race, especially in the US, is one of them, as is gender. It can also be the result of people who came before you, fighting for more access or benefits. For instance, many immigration policymakers, lawyers, or advocates paved the way for me to become a US citizen.

It can also come as a result of a life change. Say you're single when you're thirty-seven — at that point, you're not within society's norm for your age group, which is being married. But if you're married when you're thirty-eight, you've gained the privileges associated with being married.

Basically, privilege can be something you're born with, but it can also be gained.

3) Some privileges are more widespread than others

Privileges aren't limited to small groups of people. Take being a US citizen for example. The US is positioned as more powerful than the rest of the world, with more access to education and economic prosperity, and along with that comes a certain elevation in the eyes of others. And of course, there are millions of Americans.

When I was stateless and undocumented and going through deportation proceedings, I was looked down upon. But now when I flash my US passport, I'm treated much differently. Now I'm a part of a very large group of people who have the benefit of moving through the world with a higher status.

4) Everyone has it

Since privilege is so tied to context, each and every one of us can have it. All of us have at least one, and some possess two, three, or more depending on where we are. This is why understanding your own privilege is so essential to leading DEI efforts within an organization — acknowledging that we all are at an advantage at one point or another is an equalizer. Starting from the same place of understanding is a great place to begin your DEI efforts in earnest.

Why Understanding Privilege Is Key to DEI Success

Seeing how we're similar is a great jumping off point for becoming aware of the biases that prevent DEI from flourishing. Once you're aware of your advantages, you can openly discuss them, use that knowledge to address your biases, and work towards breaking the cycle of exclusion.

Here's a further breakdown of how understanding privilege can create a more equitable workplace:

1) Recognizing that we all have privilege creates self-awareness

Just by acknowledging what privilege is and reframing it like we did above, we can diffuse all of our triggers. We won't immediately go on the defensive if someone points out an advantage we have, but instead, we can reflect on all of our layers of diversity. We can see that just because we have certain advantages doesn't erase any of the pain we've felt or the hard work we've done.

In the process of disarming these triggers, we have the opportunity to realize that we're not in an "us" versus "them" dichotomy. After all, that doesn't tie back to DEI, because DEI is about being inclusive and inviting everyone into the conversation regardless of who they are.

If we say that only one group, like white people or men or wealthy people, has all the privilege, then we're not being very inclusive. That ends up being more damaging that anything else, especially in the workplace.

We also deny ourselves of our voice, which is our source of power and dignity. We can only change things when we don't feel victimized by them. In order to do that, we need to recognize the power that we have in the situation. We only hurt ourselves when we choose not to recognize our power, even if it's miniscule. In this case, we benefit DEI by recognizing our privilege, no matter who we are.

When we understand privilege, we can have constructive conversations and ask ourselves, well, what are our privileges? How do we become more aware of them? What can we do to become better allies to those who don't possess privilege in those areas? And what does it mean to have access to a certain space, community or environment that someone else might not have?

Asking ourselves these questions can help us break down how our benefits affect our work, ultimately helping us understand how our benefits affect our biases.

2) Self-awareness of our privilege can help us mitigate our biases

Once you start unpacking your own privileges, you might start to realize just how much of an impact they've had on your life, and how you've created a certain filter that didn't allow you to feel or see the experience of someone who doesn't have the same benefits. Basically that filter has likely led you to be unintentionally exclusionary.

Here's an example. Say you were interviewing someone who went to the same Ivy League university you graduated from. That can become an affinity bias because you might think, "I know people who come from that university — they're always smart." Maybe that's the case, but maybe it's not.

After that, you interviewed someone from a university that isn't considered particularly prestigious. You may not feel a connection to them and may not realize that your affinity bias is the reason why. Instead, you might think that because they didn't go to the university we went to, they aren't a good fit for the position.

What we don't realize is that we're being exclusionary. Our bias is influenced by the privilege of going to an Ivy League school, and in order to attend that school, we likely had other privileges such as our upbringing, parents, and environment.

However, the person you interviewed who didn't go to an Ivy League school may be just as intelligent, but they just weren't exposed to that university as a possibility based on their access to money and scholarships, or their upbringing. In this instance, your biases may have steered you away from someone who was a great fit for the role.

When we look at resumés, we create two stories: who we think the candidate is and who we think is the right fit for the position. Both stories limit us. We don't know enough about a candidate from a resumé to make judgments, yet we still use that as a baseline to hire the candidate even before we interview them.

Think about how many times you might have glanced over a resumé and picked up on a few items that you liked or didn't like and had a 'hunch' about the applicant. You're not alone — a study from Harvard Business Review showed that 60% of hiring managers know whether they'll hire someone within the first fifteen minutes of meeting a candidate.

If you had stepped back and taken a look at the privileges you had, asking yourself why you feel the way you felt about the candidate who went to your university, you could have made your hiring decision based on qualifications instead of feelings that you didn't fully analyze.

But on the flip side, say you did hire the person from a less prestigious school. The way your biases could affect them don't end once they've accepted the job offer. Your biases could affect how you evaluate their performance and even your willingness to promote them. Alternatively, as they move through the ranks, you can continue to reflect on how your privilege has influenced your biases.

Does the person from the less prestigious university have the same access to sponsors, mentors and programs to continue to build their skillset and become eligible for a promotion? Are there any lingering biases that are preventing you from seeing this person on an equal footing as someone who went to a more well-known school? Examining your own privilege and fighting against your own biases is an ongoing process.

I am not suggesting that having an affinity to someone's background — like playing intramural sports or being from the same town — is bad. What I am suggesting is that you should look for the connection to the skills required for the position. For instance, if you notice that someone is a ballet dancer and you think highly of ballet dancers, that's not a good enough reason to advance the person in the interview process. However, if you are able to conclude from their interview that dancing takes discipline and a requirement of the open position is discipline, then it makes sense to take an interest in that applicant based on their dance background.

The more you get used to looking at yourself and understanding how your benefits have shaped the lens that you view others through, the more you can break down the biases that prevent everyone from getting a fair opportunity.

Sometimes, people misinterpret this as a push for quotas. Diverse slate hiring is not about quotas. Instead, what I am suggesting is that managers cast the widest net of qualified applicants to increase their chances of finding the best talent out there, which will most likely be diverse across different categories.

3) Mitigating our biases can break the cycle of exclusion

Once I was leading a session and asked each person to really examine their own privilege. What was great was that each person was able to acknowledge that this was hard, like putting a mirror up to their face, and that sometimes, privilege can be generational.

For instance, if someone grew up in a family where multiple generations never went into tech or another high-paying field, they're less likely to have access to the tools that can help them get into tech. But if we open up our candidate pools, internship programs, and mentorship opportunities to those people, we can break that cycle.

Getting a clear picture of our privileges and asking ourselves how we relate to others who may not have those advantages can help us see how privilege can be cyclical. We can begin to understand the systemic infrastructures that perpetuate discrimination in the workplace and outside of it, and we can influence change in our own way, especially as managers.

The conversation about privilege goes hand in hand with equity. Every employee doesn't enter the workplace with the same experiences and opportunities, and that's why workplaces have an opportunity to level things out and create more fairness. But understanding how we've benefitted isn't the same as taking action. Next, we'll tackle scenarios where we need to take heed of our privilege, and how to have conversations around DEI that create positive change.

Exercises for Chapter #3

Your Turn:

Identify one diversity category where you possess privilege and consider how you have benefitted in your life experiences based on that privilege:

Diversity Categories:

- Race
- Ethnicity
- Ableness
- Gender
- Sexual orientation
- Education
- Color
- Nationality
- Marital status
- Military status
- Religion
- Socioeconomic
- Age
- Language

Take it to Your Team:

We know that equitable practices help to address imbalances around privilege. As a manager, you can begin to establish equitable practices. Ensuring that your direct reports have a mentor or sponsor, have equal access to senior leadership, and can participate in training and development programs are just some ways to provide them with resources to grow within the organization. Do one or all of the following:

1. Once a quarter, invite a senior leader to have a round table discussion with your team on current business. If you do this, make sure all members of your team have an opportunity to introduce themselves to the senior leader and are prepared/can pose a question so they get exposure.

2. Walk your team through the benefits of having a mentor or sponsor, and encourage each one to identify a mentor inside the organization or externally.
3. Make sure that all members of your team are aware of, and feel like they are allowed to carve out time, to participate in training sessions and other personal development opportunities. If they don't, encourage it and help them to make time for professional development.

CHAPTER FOUR

Courageous Conversations

Now that we have a clear understanding of privilege and how it leads to biases, we can dive into the specifics of how to assess our privilege in common workplace situations and have effective conversations about DEI without fear.

Navigating situations where privilege plays a part is key to being a successful manager, and it's vital in influencing DEI change within an organization, and by extension, within society. As we covered in chapter two, a manager can motivate or de-motivate an employee, and including DEI in your everyday work life can help those in under-represented groups feel welcomed. The entire company can improve from the change.

Being aware of your benefits (or privileges) isn't necessarily about giving up your authority as a manager in order to make people feel comfortable. You've earned that position and have to manage your team in order to reach whatever objectives your role entails. It's about being able to differentiate between your authority and your privilege. This isn't something you can just think about once and move on from — you have to constantly evaluate it depending on the circumstances you're in.

Assessing your privilege at work can be split up into two categories:

1. Your privilege in relation to your direct reports (especially in regard to their sense of belonging, feeling of being valued, productivity, and how they're perceived) and to other managers. Since you are their superior, you possess a greater sense of belonging to the organization than your

direct reports and it's your responsibility to extend an invitation.

2. How your privilege affects your output in terms of the product or services you provide to customers or clients.

Your Privilege in Relation to Other Managers and Your Direct Reports

As I explained in chapter three, we all have our privileges, which can expose us to environments that form our sense of what's normal and, by extension, lead us to form biases that shape the way we see the world. If we show up at work without having acknowledged those privileges, we can perpetuate biases that can make our team or our fellow managers feel less able or less motivated to do their best work.

Let's break down situations where our privilege could play a factor, and what questions to ask ourselves to ensure we're bringing everyone into the conversation.

Accessibility

Managers have the power to present people on their teams with more access to opportunities to integrate them into rest of the organization, especially people who might feel isolated or disconnected from the others.

Because they can open these doors, managers can also be more vigilant in observing people's talents and offering them more developmental opportunities. This can help lead to career advancement which can also lead a person to feel more valued in an organization. Managers should recognize where their subordinates might lack privilege and help them navigate.

Being able-bodied, for example, is the norm in society. Managers might not think about how that privilege can lead them to exclude people who aren't in that group. Disabilities can be physical, mental, or developmental, and taking the time to put yourself in those peoples' shoes can go a long way in creating an inclusive atmosphere.

For instance, say you're delivering a workshop and looking for virtual platforms to deliver those trainings. If you're an able-bodied person, you might not necessarily consider what it could be like for someone hearing-impaired or blind to access those workshops because being able-bodied is just so innate to your life experience. If you leave your privilege unchecked and feel like adding closed captions or some other feature to make it easier for visually impaired people to participate is an inconvenience, you won't get the value of having those peoples' perspectives.

But we're here to learn how to be more inclusive managers. In a situation like the one above, or at any other time where you're going to be creating a workspace or planning a meeting, ask yourself:

- Are there any individuals who might not have access to this meeting or opportunity?
- If so, how can I work around that? How can I find the right tools to facilitate an environment that's inclusive for everyone?

Meetings

Meetings give us the opportunity to think about our privilege and about those in a room who may not share the same benefit. While we can't speak for every group, we can call out the fact that some groups don't have as much representation as others, or create awareness that a valuable perspective might be missing. Just being openly aware of your own privilege can help you make others aware of theirs as well.

For example, say you're in a meeting about a new initiative in your company, one that could potentially benefit everyone. However, everyone in the meeting is male. If you're a man who's aware of his privilege, you can mention this and try your best to think about how a woman may feel about what's going on. Like I just said, we can't speak for every group, but awareness can go a long way in making things more inclusive.

We also get to be an ally to those who are under-represented or advocate for their ideas. A great example of allyship that I personally experienced within the last three years was when I was invited to consult an organization. One of the senior leaders was not too keen on the workshops on race because they were concerned about how it could be misinterpreted, or how it could lead to legal ramifications. They started raising their voice and really pushing me, not allowing me to finish my train of thought.

And I was the only black person and person of color on the call. I started to feel overwhelmed and explain my rationale, but I wasn't getting through. Another senior leader, a white male, stepped in and said he supported me and that they brought me in because I was a valuable expert.

That felt so amazing to me because this person noticed that I might not have been comfortable. It's absolutely true that part of my job as a consultant is to be challenged, but this man supported me when things were becoming tense. He didn't speak for me — he just let me and everyone else know that he had my back.

In a meeting where you see that there are under-represented groups, or feel that someone isn't being supported, ask yourself:

- How can I be a good ally for this person?
- Is there someone without a certain privilege being invited to the table to speak?
- How can I amplify their voice instead of speaking over them?

Delegating

Managers delegate tasks all the time, so recognizing your privilege while assigning things can go a long way in creating a more equal environment. Just as we talked about hiring and being able to differentiate between gut feelings about a candidate and their ability to do a job, we can do the same for delegating.

Consider the following:

- Is the way in which I've determined someone's ability to do a job clouded by my privilege? For instance, am I choosing one report because he has a similar educational background instead of looking at each report's abilities alone?
- Am I delegating tasks evenly, or are some people getting more projects or opportunities than others?

Problem-solving, decision-making and brainstorming

In chapter one, we talked about how increased diversity can lead to better problem-solving, stronger decision-making, and increased productivity. Understanding your benefits can help you reap all the benefits of a diverse set of perspectives, but we have to be very deliberate in how we get those points of view and make our decisions.

We need to be truly open to people providing different creative solutions, and make sure that we listen to understand, and listen from a point of compassion and empathy, two things we'll get into later in this chapter. I encourage managers to give people permission to have a dissenting point of view.

Since our direct reports are our subordinates, they might not feel safe in going against us in fear that there will be repercussions down the line. If we start by telling them that we welcome differing opinions, they won't feel as if they're walking into a trap by expressing themselves.

Once you've created an environment where people feel comfortable sharing their opinions, you can assess your privilege again to ensure that you've truly included everyone, then make decisions that truly encompass a variety of perspectives.

Ask:

- Does anyone have a dissenting point of view, or would anyone like to play the devil's advocate?
- Have I heard from everyone on the team?
- Are we missing a perspective that could help us get to a better solution?
- Is everyone represented in the decision-making, or are some people weighing in more than others?

Your privilege and the work you do

The impact of our biases goes beyond the people we work with and affects the work that we put out, whether we're working with other businesses or consumers. Without understanding how your privilege creates blind spots, it's easy to miss out on opportunities that can include new customers or make your client base feel like you see them.

One example that comes to mind is Apple's HealthKit, which was initially rolled out in 2014. The app promised to monitor your weight, your medications, your food intake, exercise, and any other health metric you could think of…but not reproductive health. To anyone with a menstrual cycle, this felt like a no-brainer to include data points to measure your reproductive health.

Apple was mostly white and male at the time, and even though they asked a number of physicians when developing the app, they still had this massive blind spot that pushed people to select apps developed by competitors. Situations like this really drive home the impact of considering privilege and other perspectives when creating consumer products. If Apple had been as inclusive as possible when working on the app, they could have won over more users from the beginning.

When coming up with products, branding or marketing materials, consider:

- What's our customer base — what do they look like and who are they? If they're a business, who are their employees?
- Are we mirroring the population of our customer base in our marketing and promotional materials? Or are we just focused on the mainstream and the people who we see in our company?
- Have we gotten feedback from under-represented groups, including dissenting points of view?

This list of scenarios and questions is by no means exhaustive, but it's a great place to start curbing the negative effects unchecked bias can bring, and creating a more inclusive environment for the people you work with and the customers you serve.

What Does a Constructive DEI Conversation Look Like?

Conversations about diversity, equity, or inclusion can start in a number of ways. One of your direct reports might reach out to you and say they experienced a microaggression, or they might tell you that they don't feel welcome. Or you might encounter a situation where someone doesn't feel comfortable with their team.

There are ways in which you can try to tackle DEI issues, but end up alienating the person who came to you instead. For instance, I once approached a manager I had about a microaggression I experienced from a team member, months after it happened. Instead of responding in a way that made me feel heard, my manager said, "Well, why didn't you tell me before? I would have supported you. I wish you would have said something."

While she likely didn't intend to make me feel bad, I ended up feeling that I was in the wrong and she was in the right for suggesting that I come in sooner. I went on the defensive, which defeated the purpose of coming to talk to her about it. I started to feel like I shouldn't come to her with issues like this, instead of coming away from the issue having an active ally in my corner.

Part of the challenge is that we sometimes respond to DEI issues like they are connected to harassment and involve legal action. Our responses can come off as mechanical and disingenuous because we fear legal ramifications. There are instances where DEI-related complaints are tied to harassment. But most times, DEI concerns can be subjective and don't necessarily require legal action. Those instances should be handled with a level of empathy.

Every situation is different, but there are a few guidelines to follow during these conversations:

1) Open with a disclaimer

HR departments have certain protocols that are absolutely critical in situations like these, which you should bring up before you start collecting information about what happened.

If you aren't familiar with the specifics, open the conversation by saying something like, "There are certain guidelines that we have to follow in situations like this, and if what you tell me meets certain criteria for harassment, I can't keep it confidential and have to share it with HR." Opening with this will ensure that both of you are on the same page, and the person who comes to you won't feel as if you've betrayed their trust in reporting the situation.

Secondly, tell them that you'll do your best to understand as much as you can. Of course, not everyone has experienced or will experience certain microaggressions, but the next step will help you begin to put the pieces together.

2) Ask permission to ask questions

Your first instinct might be to ask them what happened, but don't. Starting a conversation by asking someone questions will make that person feel like they're in an interrogation and not a conversation, like you're suspicious of them or their motives.

Instead, ask permission to ask questions. It starts to build more trust between you and the person who's come to you and sets up the foundation for a conversation based on understanding rather than agreeing or disagreeing.

3) Ask clarifying questions

Now that you've asked for permission to ask questions and established trust, you can start gathering information about the specifics of the situation. Where did it happen, and how did it make that person feel? Again, this is about listening and understanding as much about this person's experience as possible. The next step will help you to do this.

4) Look for evidence as to how this person is like you

As you listen, think about the ways in which this person is like you. As we've discussed, there are a lot of things that make us more similar than we are different. In fact, assume that this person is like you and look for evidence of this. For instance, maybe one of you is an Asian woman and the other person is a black man, but both of you might be in the LGBTQIA+ community and know how it feels to be in that non-dominant group. Understanding each other is a great place to begin validating this person's feelings.

5) Validate

Validation doesn't mean that you're agreeing with someone or taking their side. It's more like saying something simple like, "I hear you," or "I understand the pain you're experiencing." It allows people to feel safe and that they're not alone. This further establishes trust and creates an environment where these feelings can be openly shared without fear.

People have often told me that they're nervous at the idea of someone coming to them for something like this because they can't "fix" the problem. But fixing the problem is actually the worst thing you can do. Most of the time, people just want to be heard and accepted.

6) Next steps

Of course, if someone reveals that they're being harassed, or that someone else is creating an unsafe work environment for them, then bring the situation to HR.

If the situation doesn't need to involve HR, you can simply ask, "How can I support you? What would be the best next step?" You'd be surprised at the answers — most of the time, the person will probably say that they just appreciate you allowing them to share what had happened. They were looking for that validation.

Discussions Where You've Been Accused of Bias or Are the Target of Bias

Not every conversation about DEI will feel like the ones above. Sometimes, we might be in conversations where someone says we're being biased, or we'll feel that we're the target of bias. This could be very triggering, automatically putting you on the defensive. If you're feeling unsafe or, or in other words, that you feel unable to be physically, mentally, and emotionally present, then remove yourself from the situation. The same goes for when you feel like you're at risk of losing it.

When we're accused of something, we're quick to think about how it's an attack on our character and go on the defensive. If someone says something that reminds us of a bad experience we had, or does something that brings up an emotion, we become fearful.

What I encourage you to do in either situation is to stay engaged. When we're in these situations, we'll probably want to stop but, if you're just uncomfortable, keep going. Like I said in the beginning, discomfort is where we grow as managers and team members.

Instead of removing ourselves from the conversation, we should think about how this person is like us, just as we would do if someone else brought a discrimination issue to our office. When we relate to each other, we can diffuse those triggers and start the discussion from a more empathetic place.

The next step is familiar by now — ask clarifying questions and listen to understand instead of to win. In these conversations, you or someone else is being accused of not understanding, and this gives us the opportunity to ask open-ended questions. When we ask open-ended questions instead of questions that can be answered with a simple yes or no, we allow a person to talk and share more of how they feel.

Sometimes it's less about not agreeing with the other person and more of our lack of understanding. For instance, microaggressions are personal feelings about a comment or action that are tied to a group affiliation. We will explore microaggressions in greater detail in chapter six so we will start with an example for now. Complimenting a Black woman by telling her that she reminds you of Michelle Obama might be offensive to them. While they might respect and admire Michelle Obama, some would feel like you were suggesting all Black women look alike.

If you were the one who said that, you may not understand how someone could be offended by what was seemingly a compliment. If their explanation doesn't help you to better understand, there's another option. Simply ask, "How could I have said it differently or better?" Their response might be, "I would much rather the compliment about my character first, which illustrates to me that you are observing me and not simply comparing me to one of the few Black women you might be familiar with."

Allowing someone to speak freely ties in to our goal of finding how the other person is similar to us, rather than focusing on what makes us different. The more we know, the more similarities we can find.

There are a couple of theories about what we're looking for when we listen to understand, and one is position versus interest. This is actually a common negotiation tactic. While people might have different positions on an issue, particularly when they're in an argument, they usually have the same interest.

For instance, my position on baking a cake might be to put in four cups of sugar, but yours might be to include three and a half. We have different positions on the issue of how to bake the cake, but we're both interested in baking a delicious cake. So, when we're searching for evidence as to how we're similar to one another, we're actually looking for our shared interests in this disagreement or discussion.

You get to say something like, "Look, I know this is a heated conversation and we have differing opinions, but I know there's something we must agree on. We have to figure that out."

Figuring out your common interest is one of the most important things in these conversations — what are we agreeing on in terms of gender or race, or being at work, as it relates to DEI? Maybe that shared interest is that we think all people should be treated fairly and equal in the workplace. Finding that shared interest can diffuse the strong emotions that could actually create more strife and division. We want to unite instead of divide.

In addition to thinking about positions versus interests, we want to think about intention versus impact. I love to use the example of when you're arguing with your significant other. You tell them that they hurt your feelings when they said something, and they reply with, "Well, that wasn't my intention." How does the argument go? The answer is that it probably continues, or the other person harbors more resentment even after the argument ends.

That frustration builds because the argument hasn't been resolved — when we hide behind our intent, we don't validate that person's feelings. That's not what gives them peace and comfort that their feelings were truly hurt. If we acknowledge someone's feelings, telling them that we understand and hear them, we can help them release them and lower the tension.

You have to fist pivot your focus to the impact of your words or the words that were said to you. Once you've validated those feelings, you can tell them that it wasn't your intention.

We should also think about reacting versus responding in scenarios like this.

Reacting is very much about words — like a tweet sent from a corporate account or an Instagram post after something happens. It's short-term and can't really scale into anything bigger or long-lasting because they haven't thought about the actions that need to go behind those words. It's like looking at a symptom on the surface, but not a cause. When we fix the symptom, we don't actually get at the root of the problem. It's a quick-fix, and as I mentioned in chapter one, DEI isn't something that can be implemented overnight.

Responding involves a lot more understanding, unpacking, and learning. It's like getting to the root of an illness instead of just putting a Band-Aid on it. We have to constantly do the work to see how we've formed the biases or privileges that we have, and how those things affect everything we do.

So, when we're in a situation where we're being accused of a microaggression or some other offense, we don't get to hide behind, "That wasn't my intention." We have to focus on the impact and say, "I'm sorry, I'm hearing this," before explaining why what we said wasn't what we intended to say. From there, we get to respond by trying to understand how something was offensive or how we can do better in the future.

The steps above are also great examples of active allyship. Let's take a closer look at what that means.

Your Turn:

You have a private conversation with a recently hired 50-year-old male who expressed a feeling of resentment at the dismissive attitude and tone in team meetings by a 30-year-old about the elder's lack of experience with high tech applications. Write out your talking points or statement for all five steps.

Step #1- Give a Disclaimer

> *Example: Before you reveal any information, I want to be transparent with you and let you know that I take your feelings seriously, and anything you share that suggests that anyone is at risk or a subject of harassment has to be reported back to Human Resources.*

Step #2 - Ask for Permission to Ask Questions

Step #3- Ask Clarifying Questions

Step #4 - Look for Evidence of how this person is like you:

Step #5 – Validate:

Take it to Your Team:

For your next team meeting, or when you next delegate tasks, select at least one of the questions below to pose to your team members.

The purpose of this exercise is to remember how different forms of diversity influence our experiences and perspectives, which transfer into the workplace. We get to widen our point of view or lens by hearing from others. This not only creates more inclusivity, but it creates a greater sense of belonging.

1. What would a dissenting perspective be on this initiative?
2. Whose perspective is missing in this conversation that represents our population or our clientele?
3. What are your concerns? If a person had objections about this process what could they be?

CHAPTER FIVE

Active Allyship

In the wake of the killing of George Floyd, I spoke with a C-suite executive at a company, giving them feedback on how their company had responded to the event. They seemed to understand, agreeing with what I was saying, but then they pivoted and asked me, "Why don't you put together proposals we can do to address this?"

This is the perfect example of passive allyship. Just the name itself makes it clear what it is - you aren't actively supporting and validating people in marginalized groups. When we look at the history of diversity efforts in corporations, we can attribute some of the lack of change to this backseat approach.

On the other side, there's active allyship. I've used the term "active ally" throughout the book and you've likely picked up its general meaning from the context. But to quickly define it, an ally is someone who validates the experiences of a marginalized person, or group, in an effort to support their healing. They also partner with those groups or people to create change.

Before we get into the details of how to be an active ally, let's take a closer look into passive allyship and what passive allies look like.

1) Passive allies are not bad people

Let me say this first: a passive ally is not a bad person, villain or the culprit for all failed DEI efforts. More often than not, they actually care, but they're not taking deliberate steps to affect change.

This is often because of fear. They could be afraid of the negative repercussions of not being an ally, or maybe they simply react to an event because if they don't do something, people will look at them like they're part of the problem. An ally is usually not part of the group that they advocate for, so their lack of understanding or first-hand experience could drive fear.

In conversations about DEI, they might not want to say the wrong thing in fear of backlash and simply agree with whatever's being said, which isn't actually taking a stand for anything at all.

So, at the end of the day, passive allies are more focused on minimizing risk for themselves or their reputation, which undermines the whole idea of being an ally. It's natural to want to preserve yourself, but a big part of DEI is being uncomfortable to evolve. Being a passive ally holds you back from that growth.

2) Passive allies are disengaged

Passive allies are disengaged with the actual work of implementing DEI change, like the C-suite executive from the beginning of this section. That executive had good intentions, but they weren't taking deliberate action to engage in the process themselves. Instead, they put the burden on me as a person in a marginalized group to make the decisions, instead of approaching the situation as a collaborative effort.

Again, this can go back to fear. Someone might remove themselves from a conversation because they feel like they don't have anything to add, or they don't want to be accused of anything.

They may also stay at a distance because they don't want to seem like they're trying to dominate the conversation. I've sat in on employee resource groups at companies where managers say, "I'll just sit back and listen," or "I'm not going to help run any initiatives because I don't want it to seem like I'm taking over."

This is well-intentioned, but ultimately, it's a way of not assuming responsibility. That's been my point through the entire book so far — everyone has to be involved in saying something, especially those who are running the organization. As we'll get into when we talk about active allyship, there's a way to be involved in DEI conversations and initiatives without treading on someone in a marginalized group.

3) Passive allies can be unaware of biases, or unwilling to examine them

Like we discussed in chapter three, understanding your biases and how they affect your decision-making is key to creating an environment where everyone feels welcomed. When we don't acknowledge our advantages, we can perpetuate more passive allyship.

For instance, a passive ally might promote DEI and say that they stand for it, but they might believe that their support for DEI means that they're free from bias. And if they believe they're free from biases, they won't check in with themselves to see if they're truly being equitable in delegating, promoting, or whatever decisions they happen to be making.

Another way this passive allyship can appear is through a savior complex. This complex can be an extension of the problem of trying to rush DEI change as an organization. Basically, this person feels as if they can save someone because they believe they're in a higher standing or that they can fix it quickly rather than doing all the work. That approach can make the person being helped feel patronized, since the person isn't approaching DEI as something done between equal parties.

The 'savior' in this context doesn't see how their own biases are making them feel, as if they're superior to whatever under-represented group they believe they're trying to help. They haven't taken a step back to look at how they're helping or why.

This kind of passive allyship is more about maintaining the image and reputation as someone who's an ally, rather than truly putting yourself at risk to do the necessary work.

4) Passive allies can be a part of marginalized groups

I really want to emphasize this: being a passive ally isn't just limited to cis-gendered white men or women. *Anyone* can be a passive ally, even if they're in a marginalized group. That person or group might think, "Well, I'm a part of a marginalized group so there's nothing more to learn," or "I don't have the bandwidth or energy to teach anyone when I'm caught up in my own pain. Besides, I already live this every day."

But when we're so caught up in our own struggle, we fail to see all of the nuances of another person's diversity, or how we contribute to another group's pain. For instance, I've interacted with people who shared my first layer of diversity — our physical attributes such as our blackness — but didn't understand undocumented immigrants or stateless people, which is a part of another layer to my diversity. So, therefore, they could be part of the same community when it comes to race, but not as aware of the issues that come along with being black and of a certain immigration status.

DEI is a continuum, and not one person knows everything, or has had every experience in the world. Everyone can be an active ally to someone else in one way or another.

5) Passive allies can feel defensive

I was once speaking with a chief technical officer of a company and when I asked him, "How do you define diversity?" his answer was,

"My team is incredibly diverse." And since that was his initial statement, I knew there was a level of defensiveness there, a common trait of passive allies. We weren't going to get far until he could actually see that his definition of diversity might look different from somebody else's.

When we're not ready to look at the numbers or put the mirror in front of ourselves and acknowledge how we're contributing to a situation, we perpetuate passive allyship. It's like saying it's everyone else's problem, not our own. We have to take responsibility by taking action.

You're probably wondering what an active ally does. Let's go over that.

What Do Active Allies Look Like?

1) Active allies listen to, echo, and amplify marginalized voices

One of the most important things an active ally does is listen for someone's story without looking to be the narrator of that story or, in other words, they aren't assuming someone else's story and telling them what they think it is. Instead, they amplify that person's voice and validate their story. Validating someone else's story doesn't necessarily mean that they agree with it — it just means that they're trying to understand it to the best of their ability.

Active allies recognize that stories elicit an emotional response more than statistics or facts, creating a powerful connection. And when we sponsor or foster someone's ability to tell their own story, we reinforce those connections. We make it so someone doesn't have to stand alone as the only voice in the room.

Our response and support allows them to recognize their agency in their story, which helps them become empowered. For instance, if they've given you permission to do so, you could pivot the spotlight onto them in a meeting and give the under-represented person space to tell their story. Another example could be checking in on someone before or after a meeting and acknowledging that you'd love to hear their voice if they feel safe enough to speak.

Basically, active allies recognize that everyone has a voice and a story, but might need the reinforcement and validation to tell it. The white male executive I mentioned in the last chapter, who backed me up on a call where I was the only person of color, is a great example of this kind of active allyship in action.

He didn't try to take over the conversation and tell his colleagues what I was trying to say; instead, he noticed my discomfort and helped make space for me to speak. It was a risk for his reputation to go against the others, but that's part of being an active ally — potentially being uncomfortable and putting yourself at risk for the sake of others.

2) Active allies realize that we're all responsible for DEI change, not just people in marginalized groups

Active allies hold everyone, including themselves, responsible for the progress of DEI. They're not telling someone in an under-represented group, "Hey, now that you've brought up this issue, can you come up with a solution?" Instead, they say something like, "I appreciate your courage. Let's all come together to solve this."

They might ask the person who brought up the concern for advice on how things could be better, but they're not putting the burden of coming up with solutions on them. It's a unique dance where they don't exclude themselves from the conversation, because, as I said earlier, that's a way to not take responsibility. Instead, they make sure they're not the first person to jump in and they ask open-ended questions to hear what people have to say.

3) Active allies recognize all the layers of diversity

An active ally makes DEI inclusive of all categories and aims to not exclude anyone at the expense of including another marginalized group. It's really about making sure that everyone feels like they belong in DEI conversations and asking questions to create that kind of environment, which leads into the next aspect of being an active ally.

4) Active allies acknowledge their own biases and that they always have more to learn

Active allies know that recognizing their privilege isn't something that they only have to do once and that they have biases that need to be accounted for. They always ask permission to ask questions, then ask those questions to understand other people's perspectives. Everything is a learning opportunity for them to get deeper insight into their biases so that they can be more equitable.

Promotions are a good example of how this mindset can create a more inclusive workplace. We might like someone because they're familiar to us, whether that's because of their background or the way they look or something else. If we feel that familiarity, we might bypass or miss any errors or mistakes they make to give them a promotion based off of a gut feeling.

Another person might not feel as familiar, so we might overlook this person's positive qualities or be quick to see all of their mistakes. A manager whose an active ally would do the work to figure out where and how they might have a tendency towards one person or another, then mitigate those biases.

An active ally also gives people permission to disagree and see things differently so that everyone can grow and connect with new perspectives. I mentioned this in chapter four when I talked about how managers can recognize their privilege to foster more DEI in their workplace. For example, a manager might ask a direct report questions like, "What might I be missing in making this decision? What perspectives are we not including? What concerns do you have?" And by giving them permission to disagree with you and be open, you make them feel like they belong and that they matter. And when people feel like they belong, they typically stay and give their best.

Active allies don't have a "fix it" mentality either. They understand that this is work, and it takes time. It's something that becomes a part of their day-to-day values as a team and as a manager, which leads to DEI work being a part of the culture. We'll get into how to do this later in the chapter.

Being an Active Ally and a Manager

As we went over in chapter two, managers have the ability to be the driving force for DEI efforts across an organization. They interact with employees at every level of a company and have the ability to motivate or demotivate someone through their allyship. Just being an active ally can go a long way in creating change, but there are a few more specific tips that can improve your effectiveness as an ally/manager.

Be aware of how you present your decisions

Remember that you influence how someone perceives things, and this will have an emotional response to diversity, equity, and inclusion. Time and time again, I've heard from employees who have concerns about quotas, like whether they'll force the company to bring in lower quality employees, or whether they'll lose their job to someone in a marginalized group.

And a lot of times, a past experience has shaped this fear. Someone's manager might have told them, "I'm sorry, I would give you this promotion but I have to give it to person x for a diversity quota," or "I'd hire you for this role but we have to give it to this other person." Obviously, when you set the stage for DEI in that way, you create a negative sentiment about it. That carries in people's psyches for decades and strongly influences how they respond to DEI.

I do not think it's wise to say you chose one person over another because of DEI or because someone was part of an under-represented group. That's not fair, and that can't be a way to make decisions in a business, nor would a company condone that. First, it would be like evading responsibility towards the person who was not promoted by pushing the responsibility from the manager to the company. Second, it minimizes the value of the person who was promoted. It would be like saying they only got promoted because of whatever group they're in.

Third, it leaves everyone feeling slighted, even you as the manager. The person who wasn't promoted could resent the person who was, leading them to not value the person from an under-represented group as much. Also, it would be incredibly demotivating for the person who wasn't promoted since their hard work didn't get them to where they wanted to be for reasons out of their control.

Instead, we can frame these discussions in the affirmative. Tell your report that they're doing a great job and that it was a difficult decision, but that they are going to continue to grow and get other opportunities. Essentially, focus on actionable steps.

I think all of us have the responsibility to not take the easy route and blame diversity efforts as to why we are choosing one person to promote over another because that's only one component of a promotion decision. Again, being an active ally means taking responsibility instead of pushing the blame onto someone else.

Real change doesn't happen in trainings — it happens day-to-day

Another thing that can push people away from DEI is feeling as if it's being forced on them. They tend to retaliate or feel defensive, which undermines the whole effort. Also, you can't mitigate bias and learn to be more diverse from a ninety-minute training session. What really helps to close the gap in rolling out DEI in organizations is when everyone is responsible beyond trainings or meetings on the topic.

Let's say that your company was rolling out a product for babies and all the advertising just showed them with their moms. Using that moment to say, "Hey, we're missing a whole group of people in these ads. Who aren't we including? Is there a way to include the other people who care for babies, like grandparents, fathers, or other family members?" is far more impactful than telling people to just take notes on a seminar. This kind of active allyship seamlessly blends DEI with something a company would have done every day, rather than making it something imposed on people from the top down.

When it's a conversation and a dialogue that's facilitated with day-to-day actions, it's more scalable, and because of the wide reach that managers have, they're the best group to take this challenge on. Active allyship can become a domino effect not just within a team, but across an organization, or even multiple organizations.

Creating an Active Allyship Culture

While being an active ally as a manager is a great start, creating a culture that encourages active allyship can create even more change.

There are three ways to start building this kind of workplace:

1) Create a sense of safety

Not everyone is going to feel comfortable in the workplace, as discomfort is where you're stretched and can grow. Safety is more about knowing they could disagree with someone, or have the space to professionally express their concerns and have them taken seriously.

I know as managers we often tell our subordinates that they're allowed to ask any question, but we also have to be mindful of our actions. For instance, if we say that we're open to questions, but seem impatient when people come to us for clarification, people might not feel like they can actually come to us. Truly create that space by asking people open-ended questions and building in moments for people to share their concerns.

2) Recognize people's work

If you're recognizing people's contributions, even if their metrics or numbers aren't always hitting their targets, then you make people feel valued. For instance, if someone is the only person in a particular group, telling them their value to the overall mission can help them focus more on how they're similar to others and how they're being appreciated, which then motivates them to stay.

It doesn't have to be monetary or rewards — just letting people know what behaviors they should continue to do to contribute to the success of a business can go a long way in making someone feel like they belong.

3) Discuss the shared vision

Just like showing appreciation for someone's contributions can help people feel like they're valuable, discussing a shared mission and what everyone has in common can also reduce conflict and foster a sense of belonging.

When we create a workplace that supports active allyship, we reduce conflict. For example, if people are having a heated conversation about race or gender and feel like they belong in that conversation and are invited to join no matter what they look like, they're not as fearful. They don't feel defensive or excluded because it's a dialogue, not a debate or fight. It becomes a chance to understand each other and to work towards a shared goal.

Overall, everyone feels safer at work in a space like this, and when people feel safe at work, they're happier and more productive.

Exercises for Chapter 5:

Your Turn:

Reflect back to the last promotion you gave. You mostly likely had to choose between two people. Let's refer to them as person A and person B. Please do the following on paper, or speak it out loud. You can use this process for future promotion decisions.

A. Look for equity:

1. Look at the pay gap between person A and B. How do their current positions and levels vary? If their positions and levels are the same, what is contributing to the pay gap?

2. Compare the length of time person A and B have both been with the company and on the job.
3. Consider special projects that both person A and B have taken on. Of those, which ones did you assign to them?
4. Do person A and B have the same access to resources (mentors, visibility with leadership, etc.)? More importantly, do they each know that they have that access?

B. Look for potential bias:

1. In what ways do you feel most connected to person A or B?
2. In what ways are you most familiar with person A or B?
3. How has person A or B consistently met or exceeded the expectations of his/her/their current position?
4. How has person A or B not met expectations of his/her/their current position?
5. Make a list of how person A is equipped to perform the role of this new position.
6. Make a list of how person B is equipped to perform the role of this new position.
7. Without indicating your preference, ask cross-functional peers (who are also managers), to give their observations about the performance of person A and person B. It's important that you do not lead them or influence their opinion in any way.

C. Communication:

1. Prepare how you will deliver the news to the person who is not promoted for the position.
2. Make sure your conversation and rationale does not include the person who was chosen for the position.

3. The conversation should avoid blaming anyone or any circumstance, and it should illustrate your ownership of the decision.
4. Speak in the affirmative and ask open-ended questions about what goal and ambitions this person has for his/her/their career.

Take it to Your Team:

In your next team meeting, allocate time to discuss one question. First, explain what an active ally looks like in the workplace and provide generic examples of how an active ally can participate in promoting DEI.

Ask, "Provide one past career example where you would have benefitted from your manager or colleague acting as an active ally. How might that have impacted the outcome?"

To create anonymity, you have the option to do the following:

a. Option #1: Submit a survey or use a polling app that's truly anonymous.
b. Option #2: If you are conducting this conversation in person, have people write their responses on a piece of paper.
c. Option #3: This is the best option in my opinion. Ask a colleague who is a manager from another department to facilitate this discussion to ensure further anonymity.

Summarize results and use it as a framework for how your team can be more effective allies to one another.

CHAPTER SIX

Microaggressions

In college, I had a friend who happened to be Asian-American, Chinese-American specifically. And the first thing she said after she introduced herself to me was, "I'm not good at math, so if you're trying to be my friend just because you think I'm going to help you with math then you're talking to the wrong person."

I laughed and thought it was funny at the time, but when I look back, I think about how often she must have experienced people asking that for her to mention it right away. This type of comment is called a microaggression.

A microaggression is a subtle and unintentional comment or action towards a person who's part of a larger group. That comment is rooted in a single narrative like a stereotype or unconscious bias, leaving the target of it uncomfortable. Importantly, this feeling can vary from person to person.

In the case of my friend, people stereotyped her as being good at math and sciences because she's Asian. When people said those kinds of things to her, she was collapsed into a monolith where she wasn't allowed to have an identity. As we've discussed throughout, statements that feel like an attack on our identity are particularly impactful.

A psychiatrist and professor at Harvard, Dr. Chester Pierce, developed the concept of microaggression after observing that many of the less overt experiences and insults that African Americans faced in the US perpetuated harmful stereotypes.

The thing about microaggressions is that they're covert, not overt. And usually the person who commits that microaggression is a nice person who doesn't seem themselves as racist or sexist or discriminating in any way. But because they only know one narrative, they don't understand the ways in which people from one group can have different stories, and how misattributing a story to someone can be hurtful.

The combination of their subtlety and their weight can make microaggressions a powerful force in the workplace, making people feel alienated and isolated little by little until they leave an organization. We know that according to a Korn/Ferry study, companies across the US assume a $64 billion annual loss due to turnover related to unfairness and bias.

And while someone is in a role, these constant digs can affect someone's mental health and productivity at work. Because they're subjective, they can be hard to prove as well, which leads many to not speak up.

Since they can be hard to notice without properly understanding them as a concept, we should take a closer look at what they are and how to combat them.

A Closer Look at Microaggressions

Since microaggressions don't necessarily come from a bad place, where do they come from?

Microaggressions are rooted in implicit bias, which we explored in chapter three, and implicit bias typically stems from a lack of familiarity. A person might have developed a narrative about a certain group from an experience, situation or observation. Their observation could have come from the media or something in real life. But what matters is that the more someone sees the same story over and over again, the more it takes root in their subconscious.

Let's say you grew up watching a certain TV show that portrayed women as being catty, so that's the narrative you have about women. If you happen to be working with a woman, you might carry out a microaggression by saying, "Look, let's not be catty here," or "Let's not be crazy," when a woman voices an objection about a business initiative. You don't mean to hurt anyone — it's just the story that you've been exposed to and that presented itself through your comment.

Microaggressions can also be actions. For instance, if a non-black woman clutches their bag when a black man enters an elevator at an office, that could be considered a microaggression. It's based in the stereotype that black men are violent and dangerous. To the woman, it might be second nature, almost subconscious, but to the man, he could feel insulted because he had no intention of stealing anyone's belongings, much less a woman's purse in an office building.

One of the most difficult things about microaggressions is that the deliverer can view them as compliments, which makes it more difficult for the target to defend themselves. The deliverer could easily say, "Well, I didn't mean it like that," or "You're being too sensitive," which increases the target's feeling that their voice isn't being heard.

A good example of this is the idea of Asians being the "model minority." Like my Chinese-American friend, many Asian people are often stereotyped as being the most desirable and valuable people of color. Some people could easily think that was a compliment, but it's sort of a back-handed compliment. It overlooks the person themselves and their skillset, not allowing us to see them as an individual. We collapse them into a stereotype and we're not actually appreciating what the person has done to become who they are. It also dismisses the struggle that Asians experience in the US as a result of their race.

Microaggressions can also appear as assumptions, like assuming that someone in an administrative role is a woman, or that an immigrant can't speak English.

Another way they can appear is in someone's tone, even over email. Say a young woman emailed someone about a mistake she made that impacted a few people in other departments, though it ultimately didn't harm a lot of people. Then, an older male in a more senior position replied to her saying, "Who gave you permission to do this? Why didn't you contact me?" and copied the entire department.

If a man closer to his age had made the same mistake, there's a chance he wouldn't have responded in that way. To the woman, it might have felt like a microaggression.

Microaggressions can appear in so many different ways that we haven't covered here. The biggest takeaway is that they can be subtle and subjective, but over time, they can erode someone's sense of belonging and wellbeing at work, leading to lower productivity and higher turnover.

Microaggressions are experienced at an individual level. That means that two people who belong to the same association might hear a microaggression that's demeaning to their group. One person might be offended by what they hear, and the other might have heard this microaggression so often that they internalized it. It no longer bothers them and it's inoffensive to them. If that's not confusing, then I don't know what is!

That's why it's more important to focus on building strong relationships with your team members so that you can observe a change in their behavior, or creating an environment where your team member can share their experiences with you. When you create this type of trust with your team members, they are more likely to share what they experience in the workplace, including microaggressions. What's equally as important is how we respond.

Dealing With Microaggressions as a Manager

Now we've covered various ways that microaggressions can appear and how subtle they can be, there are also some microaggressions that are blatantly offensive but, most of the time, we won't understand when and why we have offended someone. Because of how variable they can be, you're probably wondering how to address them. The answer isn't to walk on eggshells or avoid DEI.

To put it simply, being an active ally can address microaggressions and help the targets of them feel heard. As managers, we get to look at things from the perspective of the members of our team who are different from us. Try to imagine what work would be like if you were subtly, but constantly insulted, or if you always had to defend yourself — how would that feel? It would be exhausting, right?

Managers should also reflect back to the earlier days in their career. How many of them would feel safe confronting someone who said or did something offensive? The answer is not to expect the person targeted to stand up for themselves. They might feel intimidated or worry about retaliation.

If someone comes to you with microaggressions, one of the most important things you can do is to listen and validate what someone is saying. If your response is something like, "Oh you're being overly sensitive," then you're challenging their sense of reality (sometimes referred to as gaslighting) and the target could feel dismissed and that they don't have someone in their corner. Or, if you put the full burden of proving the microaggression on that person instead of listening to their story, you end up being a passive ally by not actively engaging in conversation.

Whenever I lead discussions on microaggressions, I always have at least one manager argue that they don't agree that the individual should take offense. Situations related to bias and microaggressions are extremely personal and are felt deeply. None of us are allowed to decide what a person should be offended by, especially if we don't belong to the group that the person feels was the subject of the microaggression. The point in having someone confide in us is not to place judgment, but to coach them through a solution.

If someone does come to you after being the target of microaggressions, follow the same guidelines that we covered in chapter four on having courageous conversations about DEI — open the conversation with a disclaimer, ask permission to ask questions, follow-up with more questions to clarify, look for evidence of how this person is like you, then validate what they're saying.

Some people are quick to fear DEI because they are worried about dealing with issues like microaggressions. The truth is that microaggressions existed in the workplace long before efforts around DEI were introduced. The only difference is that, in the past, the targets of microaggressions remained uncomfortable and didn't feel like they had a voice. Now, everyone in the workplace bears a responsibility for microaggressions in the workplace. We are all uncomfortable on our way to developing a more inclusive organization.

If you get into the habit of exercising your ally muscle and pivoting your lens to see from other people's perspectives, you might notice more microaggressions. In this case, speak up — after the fact, go up to the person who was targeted and ask, "Were you impacted by anything that was said in that meeting, or did anything come across as offensive? I want to make sure that no one felt unwelcome in that situation."

Or, if someone is being targeted, you can back them up and wait for them to speak.

I cannot tell you how many times an active ally speaking up for somebody or having their back has really taken the weight off of an under-represented person. It's a big part of creating a safe environment where everyone feels welcome, and by setting the example, more of your team will feel comfortable addressing microaggressions as well. Make it a team effort and let people know that they can come to you if they're having a problem.

But what if you're the person who wants to say something to someone that could be perceived as a microaggression? You can approach it like a productive DEI conversation by opening with a disclaimer, creating context, and asking for permission.

Here's an example. Say you're a person from an under-represented group who passes as white and you want to ask a person of a different ethnic group where they're from during a networking event. This could come across as a microaggression because you could be implying that they're not really from the US or that you're putting them in a different category than yourself. You could start with a disclaimer to explain the context for why you're asking the question, like, "Even though I'm from XYZ country, I now live in an area that isn't as diverse, so I'm always drawn to people with multicultural backgrounds."

That starts diffusing the potential tension, as the person understands where you're coming from. Afterwards, get permission to ask them the question you had in mind with a simple, "May I ask you something?" If they say yes, ask them about their last name. So the key here is context to avoid having something come across as a microaggression.

As I said earlier in the chapter, microaggressions are subjective and experienced personally. It's not up to us to agree or disagree on whether or not a person should be offended. We are not part of the group or association that the recipient of the microaggression is a part of. Therefore, we won't understand the history and connotation of our words and actions in the same way that they will experience it. It's futile to try to play judge to determine if something is a microaggression or not.

I'm also not suggesting that we tip-toe around everyone and refrain from speaking. The point that I am making is that at some point we are bound to say or do something that someone doesn't agree with. If we focus on trying to avoid microaggressions, we are likely to fail. Certainly, there are microaggressions that are blatant and obvious, but many are not. The key is to create a space to listen and understand the person affected. As managers, we want them to feel safe enough to tell us what hurts them. This level of validation goes a long way with dealing with microaggressions.

How Your Direct Report Can Deal With Microaggressions at Work

Since anyone can be the target of a microaggression, it's important to know how to handle them in the workplace.

First, decide whether you feel safe or unsafe in a conversation, because if you feel unsafe, you'll want to remove yourself from the situation. Don't further engage — just say something like, "It seems like we're both very passionate about what we're talking about and maybe this is a good time for us to take a pause and revisit it once we've both cooled off."

But if you do feel safe, you want to assume that this person isn't trying to hurt you. They just have a limited perspective, or their comment is based on a limited narrative. Once you've made that decision, you can ask them to elaborate.

A workplace microaggression against BIPOC, especially black people, is that they're very articulate. I've been faced with this microaggression in the past. This could be offensive because it's rare to hear people of other races getting that compliment as frequently, as if they're not expected to be articulate. Once when I was in this situation, I asked that person what they meant.

They said that they meant I was animated in the way I spoke, and that I used simple language that everyone, from the most educated person in the room to the least educated, could understand. They thought that the way I spoke invited everyone in, regardless of who they were.

In asking this person to elaborate, I got more clarity and understood that he didn't mean to say what I thought he was saying. When we're the recipient of microaggressions, we shouldn't be so quick to label the person. When we do, they become defensive and it becomes a back and forth instead of a true conversation. So, ask more open-ended questions like, "Can you explain what you mean by that?" or "Can you elaborate?"

If you still feel that they're delivering a microaggression, add in a disclaimer like, "I don't know if this is what you're trying to convey, but I'm hearing X," and explain what you're hearing. Most of the time, what we heard isn't what the person is trying to say. But if you're both feeling frustrated, stop the conversation and revisit it later.

But, usually, once you've asked those questions, there's clarity and you realize that it was literally a matter of miscommunication and nothing more.

Generally, handling microaggressions with grace as either a manager or a recipient of a microaggression, or both, comes down to open communication. By being willing to listen and ask questions, we can form deeper connections with one another and foster an environment that makes everyone feel welcome. We can also deepen our connections by understanding stereotypes and the tropes and biases that result from them.

Your Turn:

Consider how you would respond to your direct report who approached you with any of the below scenarios. Hint: your response should involve a coaching conversation.

Your Direct Report's Identity	Category	Behavior	Interpretation
Woman	Sex	In every meeting, even the ones that she sets up, her male colleague speaks first, talks over her and cuts her off.	She feels like her male colleague is dismissive because she's a woman.
Non-binary	Gender	Their cisgender colleague uses she/her pronouns rather than they/them.	They feel as if their gender identity is being disregarded.
27-year-old man	Age	His older male colleague likes to give him unsolicited advice about the job because he's younger.	He feels like his colleague, who is visibly older, talks down to him because he's young.

Mexican-American woman	Race	Her colleague tries to reassure her after a training session on racism by saying, "Look, I don't see color. I think everyone should be treated the same."	Her colleague makes her feel invisible because of her race.
A man dealing with mental health	Ableness	He constantly hears his peers make exaggerations like, "I'm so OCD," or "She's so bipolar," to emphasize a point.	As a person who experiences mental health, he doesn't appreciate jokes about it.
A Russian man	Nationality	His co-workers tell him they're surprised he smiles and that he's not like other Russian people.	He feels as if he's being unfairly categorized as serious and unfriendly.

Take it to Your Team:

Directions: Now that we know that our success in navigating DEI conversations, including microaggressions, is based on forging open and honest communication with our teams, consider how you can do that more effectively. Here are some steps you should consider when building trust with your team members.

1. Are you scheduling weekly or bi-weekly meetings with each team member?
2. Ask your direct reports the following questions and then apply their responses:
   a. How do you like to receive feedback?
   b. What do you think your communication style is?

    c.   What is something that your former manager or professor did to garner your trust?

    d.   What's important for me and the team to understand about your work style?

3.   Ask your direct report about areas or skills they want to develop, and work collaboratively to create stretch assignments.

4.   At the end of each weekly or bi-weekly meeting, set aside 10 minutes to discuss your direct report's performance, starting with positive reinforcement and then areas of opportunity.

5.   Get in the habit of asking your direct report to provide feedback about you.

6.   Schedule meetings with your direct report or your entire team outside of a traditional office. Go to a local coffee shop or go for a walk. If you meet in the office, change the balance of power and have your direct report sit at the head of the table or schedule meetings in his/her/their office if he/she/they have one.

CHAPTER SEVEN

Understanding Stereotypes, Tropes and Tokenism

Growing up, I went to a prep school where I befriended a lot of students from South Korea. They always said I was so nice and sweet, and I didn't understand why they seemed so surprised by that.

They told me that I was different than the black person they had seen in the media. On TV, they always saw black people doing violent things, and assumed that I would be similar.

This wasn't a conscious bias, it was an example of how having a single narrative about a group of people can lead to stereotypes and tropes, an idea we'll explore shortly. I was one of the only black people they'd met in their lives, so it isn't surprising that they'd internalized that message.

If I happened to be angry or violent, I would have just fed into the belief they had but, because I wasn't like the stereotype of black people my South Korean friends had seen in the media, I had the opportunity to reshape and undo that stereotype, or at least make them see me as an exception to it.

At the end of the day, it was up to them to choose to see me as an exception to the rule or dismantle the stereotype in their head now that they knew it was just that — a stereotype.

This is why recognizing and understanding tropes, and one of their consequences, tokenism, is important for the workplace. If we don't see tropes and stereotypes in our everyday lives, we won't see how we can unintentionally create an environment that alienates (or tokenizes) people, even in our attempts to bring more diversity into our organizations.

In order to understand how stereotypes, tropes, and tokenism are linked and make people in under-represented groups feel unwelcome, we should start by defining each term.

Stereotypes, Tropes, and Tokenism

Stereotypes

Out of the terms I've introduced in this chapter that you're probably the most familiar with is stereotypes. Stereotypes are beliefs that we have about a group's characteristics or behaviors that are based on a single or limited perspective. There are stereotypes about every group out there, and you've likely been stereotyped at some point in your life.

The thing about stereotypes is that we often have evidence to support that stereotype, whether that's because we interacted with someone in the group who happened to be the stereotype, or because of what we've been exposed to in our environment. But the evidence that we have is often based on one experience or limited experiences, which isn't an accurate representation of a group.

Stereotypes can lead to biases, which can then lead to microaggressions. Neither are conscious attempts to exclude or discriminate against people, but they do impact how we interact with them. When we have one narrative about a group of people, that changes how willing we are to interact with that group. As a result, we develop certain preferences to align (or not align) with those people.

The stereotype of gay men being best friends with straight women is a good example of this. A straight woman might befriend a gay man or have more of a bias towards him because she believes he'll have certain characteristics, when, in reality, that man may not be anything close to the stereotype. He may feel as if the woman's actions or assumptions about him are microaggressions.

Stereotypes are constantly reinforced and perpetuated by our environment and, more importantly, the media. That's where tropes come in.

Tropes

Tropes are a form of stereotype that are associated with storytelling, like films, movies, TV, and the news, and they're based on a specific culture. For example, a common trope is the Uncle Tom, a black man who's seen as a sellout to white people. However, it's specific to the United States given the country's history of slavery and race relations. If someone in Germany watched a movie with a depiction of an Uncle Tom, they might not understand or even know what that means because the history of black people in Germany is different. When stereotypes depicted in film, radio and media are not limited to a specific region but are global, then they are considered to be archetypes. The Dumb Blonde is depicted in media across all cultures and is therefore an archetype.

Stereotypes and tropes have a bi-directional relationship — stereotypes reinforce tropes, and tropes perpetuate or create stereotypes. Like in the case of my South Korean friends in school, they saw depictions of black people being violent on TV and assumed that I would fit that trope and live up to that stereotype.

Another example of the connection between tropes and stereotypes is the submissive and passive Asian woman. A TV show might depict her as a smart person who never makes a ruckus in the workplace or always does what she's told. If that's the only narrative we know of Asian women, we might judge an Asian woman who doesn't fit into that trope more harshly because she's not what we expected. Our biases also come through here if we unconsciously exclude this woman because she's not fitting into the mold. This problem can have negative consequences in the workplace, as we'll get into.

The media continues to perpetuate stereotypes in the form of tropes because we've internalized them and we accept them. We watch the TV shows and we accept them because they feel real to us. And the cycle continues. If we continue to observe these tropes and stereotypes without analyzing or mitigating them, then when increased diversity at work confronts us with a related situation, we can run into tokenism.

Tokenism

Tokenism is the symbolic effort to include someone from an under-represented group who you still have stereotypes about. Often, it's not an authentic attempt to invite someone into your community or circle. Instead, it's often done in reaction to something like a diversity initiative or a world event that makes you feel that more diversity is necessary.

To do this, you might bring in someone onto your team who doesn't look like everyone else, or someone who stands out from the rest in some way, physical or otherwise. But even though you're extending a helping hand towards someone, you still have beliefs about the group this person is associated with.

Therefore, there's a level of constant judgment of this person. You'll always be comparing them to the stereotype or trope you have in your head. When we're constantly judging someone based on their group, then we're not measuring them in the same way that we're measuring everyone else on our team.

For example, pretend there's a man working at a tech company, and he's hired the first woman on his team, checking that diversity box. But he hasn't realized that he has a bias regarding women as being overly emotional and harder to work with than men. The source of the bias may be a stereotype, a trope, or family upbringing.

When this woman's performance review comes around, he judges her less on her performance and more on her personality. The criticisms that come to mind are about the times she was more emotional rather than her performance, almost as if he were confirming his own beliefs in his head. That becomes a microaggression because he's taking action based on his biases and passing her over for a promotion because he's holding her to a different standard.

As you can see from this, tokenism is a result of not mitigating biases or understanding how privilege plays a role in your decisions at work. When we don't challenge our biases and we feel pressure to create more inclusivity and diversity in our organization, we might want a quick fix.

But it's like what we discussed in chapter five — being an ally does not mean that you can fix the problem quickly by checking off a box or thinking of someone as the exception to their stereotype. We have to unpack and understand what our biases are and how internalized stereotypes can lead to us excluding people, then actively counteract that.

Some of you might be thinking that counteracting our biases by bringing in more diverse talent sounds like tokenism, but there's a big difference. Tokenism is about plugging in what you think diversity is, like adding whatever demographic is under-represented to put a bandage on the issue. Mitigating your biases naturally leads to more diversity because it's more about understanding how you contribute to biases that limit your team and organization.

Diversity doesn't just look like one of each person, as we went over in chapter three. It's a continuous process of self-analysis to ensure that our team isn't feeling tokenized. Without taking this on, tokenism can have far-reaching consequences.

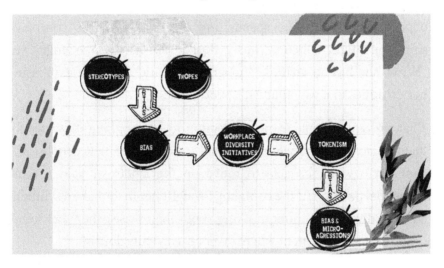

The Consequences of Tokenism

Tokenism has consequences for both the individuals who are tokenized and for managers, just like bias and passive allyship. It can alienate customers if tokenism leads to tone deaf products or messages, which then lowers a company's profitability as a whole.

Let's break down a few more reasons why tokenism is harmful in the workplace.

1) Tokenism inhibits someone's growth

Just like the woman who got passed over for a promotion at her tech company above, tokenizing someone can prevent them from growing and moving forward in a company. When we have certain beliefs about a group and haven't analyzed those biases, we continue committing microaggressions towards them through hiring, promotions, management, determining their compensation, and more.

Say a data analysis company hired a black woman for a senior level position, and she's the sole black woman at her level in that department. When she speaks and interacts with the company, someone might subconsciously think, "Gosh, she's so angry" or "Wow, she has an attitude," when, in reality, she's just expressing her critiques in a way that isn't overly nice.

That prevents people from connecting to her, making it harder for them to accept her style of leadership. A manager that people can't connect to won't be able to move up the ladder or gain a more influential position. If the company brought her in to make a symbolic effort to diversify without thinking about their biases, then they aren't creating an environment where diversity can truly flourish.

2) Tokenism makes people feel like they don't belong

As we discussed in previous chapters, feeling a sense of belonging and purpose plays a huge part in why someone stays at a company. When they feel like they fit, they're much more productive and efficient, making retention and referrals go up. If someone doesn't feel this sense of belonging, then their motivation and satisfaction go down.

The feeling of alienation that comes from tokenism can appear in a few ways. The first is avoidance. The tokenized person might feel like they have to constantly dodge microaggressions and disengage from the workplace and opportunities to move forward to avoid more things said to them that make them feel unwelcome.

An example of this is in the introduction, when I talked about being afraid to go to work. I wanted to go into my office, do my job, and go home, often making up excuses as to why I couldn't make it to office social events because I didn't want to be "othered." I felt like I stood out and wasn't truly part of the team. That definitely affected my work performance.

The second way people might react to being tokenized is feeling an intense pressure to not fall into, or reinforce, the stereotype of their group, just so they can appear to belong. After a workshop I led for one organization, a woman came up to me and said, "Martine, I can't tell you how much I appreciate you sharing and leading this conversation. There's so much pressure on me as a woman of color to not feed into stereotypes. No one realizes how much pressure it is to constantly scrutinize myself so that I don't get scrutinized by everyone else."

That kind of pressure can lead to burn out because you're constantly working hard to go against the grain and to be the ideal employee. You have to be constantly on guard and "on," which is exhausting.

The third way a tokenized person can feel like an outsider is when they're compared to the one other person in their group. If the second person in a group is constantly compared to the first person, they could be pitted against each other when they should be each other's biggest support. That sort of adversarial relationship can affect productivity and make someone feel like they're always battling someone instead of being a part of the group.

3) Tokenism perpetuates more tokenism

Sometimes when people are tokenized, they internalize and accept that as something they just have to deal with at work. Maybe they've been the target of microaggressions, or maybe they haven't had opportunities for growth that others have. Whatever it is, they've accepted it as how things are. The problem is that they perpetuate that towards another person in the same group or a different group.

For instance, if an immigrant has accepted microaggressions as a part of life at work, they might not take another immigrant's concerns about microaggressions as serious. Then, the newer person doesn't feel like they're being heard or that their feelings are valid, leading to less productivity and motivation.

4) Tokenizing prevents us from growing as managers

We've touched on this in other chapters, but when we don't try to do the work DEI requires, we hold our teams and ourselves back. Our biases could push away good employees, or not bring out the best in their work. When we tokenize people, we don't let them grow to their full capacity. We end up doing more work because we don't have a team that's working to the best of their abilities.

And ultimately, we don't actually get true diversity — we get a symbolic attempt that doesn't actually move the needle on change.

Avoiding Tokenism

Much of what we've covered in the book so far about biases and active allyship should help you avoid tokenizing someone. Do the necessary self-reflection to understand your privilege, create an open environment where your team can give you honest feedback, and do the work to mitigate your biases.

But there are two other ways to avoid tokenism:

1) Understand that we can't know about every trope or microaggression

You're not going to be able to know every trope and associated microaggression because they're deeply personal. If we're not a part of that group, we can't inspect every microaggression or stereotype. What we can do is aim to create a workplace where people feel comfortable calling out instances where someone stereotypes someone else. Fostering a culture where anyone feels like they can give you feedback, and let you know where you might be missing your biases, goes a long way in stopping tokenism.

2) Understand that judging is human nature

As much as we say we're non-judgmental, it's natural for human beings. Judging is a way to create a sense of safety in our environment by assessing everyone in it. But what we can do is accept this fact and be mindful of our advantages. We can think, "How can we mitigate these judgments?" or "How can we identify where our biases are?" instead of beating ourselves up for a natural inclination.

3) Widen your network

By taking a look at our talent pools or networks to see where there might be a lot of similarities, we can see what groups aren't being fully represented. When we decide to bring someone in from a marginalized or under-represented group, we can go out of our way to ensure that we're putting them on a level playing field and make them feel like they belong.

4) *Understand that you have to start somewhere*

As far as tokenism is concerned, we have to start somewhere in most organizations. It means that there might be instances where the first individual from a new under-represented group to the organization is sought after. The key is making sure that neither the organization as a whole, nor the people doing the hiring, focus exclusively on the person's diversity attributes. The emphasis should first be on the fact that they were hired because they met the skills required for the job. When it's not, that's when people are positioned as tokens. After the first from a particular group is hired, efforts ought to be made to ensure that they're not the sole representative from their group, otherwise that also subjects them to being tokenized. That's where diverse slate hiring comes in.

Overall, combating harmful tropes and tokenism is like a lot of DEI work — we have to reflect on our own biases, and how they can lead us to alienate others so that we can make change in the future.

Exercises for Chapter 7:

Your Turn:

Tropes and archetypes that the media perpetuate influence the stereotypes that we subconsciously carry about people. These stereotypes influence who and what we choose to familiarize ourselves with. To see how these ideas are playing in the back of our minds, identify imagery and depictions in the media that perpetuate the stereotype.

Table 2

Column 1	Column 2
Stereotype, trope and/or archetype	Identify a movie, film, cartoon or news media outlet that reinforces that stereotype
Gay men are sidekicks to straight women	
Muslims are oppressive	
Black men are violent	
Women are catty	
People from the South are not as educated	
Physically disabled people always have a superhero-like quality	

Take it to Your Team:

Dealing with stereotypes that come in the form of microaggressions or tokenism can result in a person not feeling welcomed on our team and wanting to leave. 38% of people experience bias in the workplace. Combatting this number means mitigating bias, increasing representation but also having more allies. Allyship can put pressure on both sides. It's important for all parties to understand that allies are fallible and are learning. It's also important for allies to understand where they are needed and how much they are needed.

Have your team members fill in the blanks anonymously to at least one of the three statements below. Go through and read the responses that your team offered.

Debrief by tying the conversation back to being a team and the value of understanding each other and supporting each other to achieve greater success. Supporting each other also looks like being patient with ourselves and each other in our DEI journeys.

1. If I experience ……………………….. I wish my ally would ……………………….
2. In retrospect, I could have been a better ally when …………
   ……………….……………….
3. What I wish people knew about how/why I have responded to DEI issues the way that I have is ……………………….

CHAPTER EIGHT

Mentorship and Sponsorship

Mentorship and sponsorship have benefits to both the mentor and the mentee, especially when it comes to DEI. Not only do they help more junior employees navigate through their career, but they can also positively impact both equity and diversity in a very hands-on, rewarding way.

Since the idea of mentorship is a little more common, let's start with what it is and what both parties get out of it.

Mentorship

Mentorship is a framework for a less experienced person (a mentee) to get guidance, coaching, direction and support from a more experienced person (a mentor) that helps them grow professionally. Sometimes they focus on a specific skillset or area of expertise that the mentee is interested in.

A mentee might seek a mentor whose behavior they want to emulate or who has demonstrated success that they'd also like to attain. Mentors ultimately give mentees access to things they wouldn't otherwise have, like skills, information, or certain spaces.

Also, they can help the mentee broaden their perspective and think differently, ushering them into opportunities they might not have otherwise gravitated towards because they simply weren't aware of them.

So often we think that the mentee is the only one who benefits, but mentorship is mutually beneficial. The mentor gets practice leading, managing, coaching, and building someone up, all things that are beneficial in being a manager. Since the mentee is usually younger or more junior, they can get a different perspective, think differently, and take a different approach to problems than they would have otherwise.

The mentee can also teach the mentor skills that they might not have otherwise known and, at the end of the day, mentoring is rewarding. I always tell people that you never know with your career. One day, your direct report might end up as your manager, or your mentee might be a conduit to an opportunity that could grow your career.

A critical piece of mentorship is coaching, not just training. It can be part of it, but it's not meant to be a relationship where you train them to do one thing or on a particular vocation — that's not enough. It's really about supporting someone in their development while allowing them to own it.

Here's a good example. I have a mentee, and once we were talking about how she felt stagnant in her career. She was feeling impatient about getting a promotion and moving on, so one of the first things I asked her was, "What are you looking to do? What do you want to be doing every day that you aren't already doing?"

From there, we were able to ascertain that she wanted to do more project management, which she wasn't doing at the time. I asked her follow-up questions about the skills a project manager needed and how she could develop those skills in the role she had now and on her own time. When she felt ready, I was able to support her by editing her resumé and offering her access to my network.

Essentially, mentorship is less about telling someone what to do directly. Instead, a good mentor coaches by walking their mentee through scenarios and helping them find the skills that they need.

In doing so, you're supporting them and allowing them to own their development.

Mentors can coach people within their own team, outside of their team, or even outside of their company all together. This can have a lasting impact, especially when it comes to DEI.

How Does Mentorship Reinforce DEI?

Mentorship can be a great reinforcement for DEI efforts in four key areas: improving inclusion, mitigating bias, widening our network, and increasing equity.

Inclusion

Like we discussed in previous chapters, when companies start to widen their talent pool and hire new people from under-represented groups through diverse slate initiatives, there's the risk that someone will be the only one of that group on a team. And that creates the risk of someone being "othered" or tokenized.

Having someone outside of a manager as a part of someone's support system can enhance inclusion because the mentor is making an effort to understand that person and give them a sense of belonging. Whether they identify with the group their mentee is a part of or not, mentors can be the person that their mentees go to when they have concerns that they feel intimidated to approach their manager about, or if they need an ally.

Mentors can also be allies in their mentee's promotions, performance reviews, or any situation where they need another voice there to support or guide them. They can be another person who can see your value to the organization and give you positive feedback, especially if your manager isn't giving you that support or doesn't have the bandwidth to give you individual attention.

This can foster a sense of belonging since there's someone invested in seeing you succeed within an organization.

Also, mentees from an under-represented group can find a mentor that's also from that group to support their sense of belonging. Visible representation is critical in creating a sense of belonging for all of us. It's part of human nature to seek what's familiar to us to create comfort. A mentor like this can help their mentee navigate through an unwelcoming environment, or in their upward trajectory within a company.

For instance, if there are very few people from the LGBTQIA+ community in an organization, a more junior person might seek out one of the few LGBTQIA+ individuals at the senior level for support. The mentor in this situation can give their mentee a good idea of what their career could look like, and what specific challenges they might face as someone in their community.

An LGBTQIA+ mentor could give their LGBTQIA+ mentee hope that they can progress at that company and that they're not the only one.

Like we discussed above, mentors can provide access to their mentees, and when it comes to DEI, mentors can invite their mentees into worlds that they might not have access to otherwise.

Say there's a luxury goods company where most of the employee base also has an affluent background, but someone new is from a more blue collar background. Their mentor could help them navigate and understand this new luxurious world and how to socialize within it.

For instance, golf is typically associated with affluence and could be a way for people at this hypothetical luxury goods company to socialize and make meaningful connections. But what if someone who isn't from a background where golf is played wanted the opportunity to make connections and isn't naturally invited by his peers?

In this case, a mentor could invite their mentee to play golf, introduce them to the game, and help them connect with their network. I'm not suggesting that we always assimilate, but in some cases, it can be beneficial.

Mitigating Bias

The second way in which mentorship can reinforce DEI is by helping people mitigate their biases. As I mentioned previously, mentors can be someone's advocate in situations involving promotions or new opportunities. This is also an opportunity for mentors to help mitigate bias.

Here is an example. Say some managers are meeting and talking about which team members are ready for a promotion. One name that comes up is person A's mentee, and their manager (who happens to be in the majority group) says that the mentee isn't ready for the next step.

But person A, knowing their mentee is from an under-represented group, can point out the areas in which the manager's assessment of the mentee might be clouded by bias.

Basically, mentors can not only advocate for their mentees to move forward or highlight their good work, they can also ensure that their managers are looking at their mentees objectively when the mentee might not be from the most represented group. Having a mentor who really knows the impact of the work that you do and understands your unique background can make a huge difference in someone's time at a company.

Also, a mentee might possess different attributes than their mentor, allowing both parties to widen their lens and get more exposure to other groups, therefore allowing them to mitigate their biases.

I always advise mentees to step out of their comfort zone and look beyond their natural inclinations when choosing a mentor. A more introverted person could look for a mentor who's more extroverted to hone in on skills that don't come as easily. There's always so much more to learn from someone different, and both people can see new perspectives.

Mentoring also mitigates bias by broadening someone's network. How does that happen? When someone mentors a person outside of their organization or even within their organization, they could provide someone opportunities or vice versa.

And when mentors and mentees mitigate their biases in order to connect with groups that are outside of their natural inclination, they meet people who can help them broaden their perspective and potentially their pool of talent.

Those new mentees can also introduce their mentors to groups they weren't in contact with before. For example, there are a lot of physically disabled people who are qualified for the job the mentor has. However, the mentor might not have considered them because of their lack of exposure to physically disabled people and isn't naturally inclined to look outside of his comfort zone. Having a mentee in that group can expose the mentor to great new talent.

And I'm not suggesting that every physically disabled person knows every other physically disabled person, but when we're a part of a community, we tend to know others within that community and can be a liaison between their community and yours. That can have a positive impact on the hiring process by widening the source of candidates.

Equity

When we think about equity in relation to DEI, we're thinking of two things — access and distribution of opportunities.

Accessibility to senior leadership gives people who usually wouldn't be able to be in touch with the upper levels of their company the chance to learn from them. And when we incorporate DEI practices into mentorship, we can alleviate inequity. Individuals from under-represented groups don't necessarily come into the workplace with the same support system, network, or privileges as others from the dominant group, so having the ability to connect with higher-ups can level the playing field.

Accessibility can also refer to someone's ability to access different networks in a company or field, for example, if you were a foreign national working in a US-based company. There's going to be a level of privilege that the employees from the US have that you wouldn't in that they're more culturally assimilated and familiar with the nuances of American culture. Having a mentor who's from the US, or a foreign national who has transitioned to being in the US, could give you invaluable help in navigating a new culture. That can help you catch up with your peers who might already know the ins and outs of US corporate culture.

The second aspect of equity as it relates to DEI is the distribution of opportunities. It's not just about bringing in more diverse candidates and mitigating biases, it's also about identifying where the greatest opportunities exist in the workplace. Equity through mentorship means figuring out how to give under-represented individuals exposure to areas with high growth potential.

Sometimes, companies focus on trying to add diversity to areas of the business where there's no room for real growth. This is counterproductive to DEI. Let's go through a different scenario. Say there's a mentor from a Product team, which offers more growth than other departments, and they're willing to mentor someone from other departments. Their mentorship gives their mentee entrance to a department that could offer more upward mobility, increasing diversity in higher ranks and across departments.

Sponsorship

Sponsorship has similar benefits to mentorship, but the nature of the relationship between the sponsor and the sponsored is very different. Sponsors can be at the highest levels of an organization and might have less time to coach someone or deal with the intricacies of someone's individual needs. So the sponsor really becomes an advocate.

A sponsor's focus is on understanding what your direct report's career ambitions are, and how they can help you to position your team member for future opportunities. They can also give your team members exposure to other senior leadership or situations where they might not have a seat at the table. Having a sponsor can be rewarding, but a junior employee should have a very clear idea of where they want to go and you can help prepare them.

Sponsorship can address DEI efforts through equity. When we think of systemic oppression, not everyone starts from the same playing field and some might have more hurdles to jump through in the workplace. They have less access, less privilege, and fewer benefits, all of which can impact a person's performance and upward trajectory.

There have been many instances where you hear stories of someone who was at a networking event at an exclusive club and got a job. But what if someone is working class or a single parent, or anyone else who wouldn't have access to that club?

That's why sponsorship is valuable in the workplace — it can give people who normally wouldn't have access to leadership the chance to connect with them, and that access can influence somebody's ability to get hired or promoted. A sponsor can also speak up for the less privileged in higher-level conversations, which can go a long way if a company is deciding who to let go or who to promote.

When we look at the makeup of senior leadership today, they typically look one way — they're predominantly white, cis-gendered men. Since sponsors typically come from the highest levels of a company, there are a lot of opportunities for managers to find influential sponsors and help them broaden their network and perspectives, mitigate their biases, and identify those who can be sponsored.

Creating Mentorship and Sponsorship Opportunities

In my experience working with a lot of organizations, it's very rare to come across an organization that doesn't have an organic mentorship program, meaning that they're not formalized. That makes it a limited and restricted network where a few people have mentors, and it's an unspoken understanding that some people will have this access.

Sometimes it's through nepotism and sometimes it's by having access to the people closer to the top because of the environment someone grew up in. If you're part of an under-represented group and senior level executives don't look like you or anyone in your community, how much gumption would it take to go up to that person and ask them to be your mentor? Or even consider that the person would take an interest in you? How do you even have access to that person at all?

Individuals in under-represented groups might feel insignificant in comparison to these executives, or they might not know how to ask someone to be their mentor, or even who to ask. So these programs as they currently exist in organizations only reinforce a lot of privilege.

What we get to do as managers is to help establish more mentorship and sponsorship programs on small and large scales. Here are all the ways we can do that:

1) Start with ourselves

The easiest way to start is with ourselves. We can think about where our natural tendencies lie and start to look at similarities across mentees or between our mentees and ourselves. Then, we can consider branching out to address any groups who might not know that we're offering mentorship.

2) Reach out to existing groups to see if they need mentors

Another way to branch out might be to connect to an employee resource group, a diversity council or DEI advisory group and ask if their group needs mentors or letting them know that if anyone's looking for a mentor, you're available. That's how you position yourself without making it seem like you're looking for a token or to be a savior of some sort.

Also, tokenizing someone is based on intent, and if your intent isn't about seeing someone as an exception, it doesn't become tokenism.

3) Group mentorship

Another way to incorporate DEI into mentorship is by being a group mentor. When you increase the number of people you mentor, it increases your likelihood of your mentees being diverse from each other. You can form mentorship circles where you are meeting with all of your mentees as a group. This way, you're monitoring each person and they also get to hear from each other. It's great reinforcement and a learning opportunity because it becomes a dialogue and a conversation.

4) Establish or promote existing formal mentorship programs

You can also go to human resources and ask for a formalized mentorship program, or if one already exists, ask to evaluate the distributions of partnerships across diversity lines. Just seeing where interest in mentorship lies through programs like this, or in talking to your team, can help as well. Often, the reason why there isn't a formalized program is because not everyone knows they can access a mentor or benefit from having one.

5) Mentor your direct report

Lastly, you can be a mentor to your direct report. This is less common because there's a conflict of interest; a mentee may not feel comfortable disagreeing with, or divulging information to their mentor if they're also their manager. This method only works if the manager establishes real trust with their direct report.

If you decide you want to mentor your direct report and you establish trust and open communication, that's a great place to start. If you have a group of people and you don't have the bandwidth to be a mentor to them all, you can create a mentorship circle and reinforce inclusion for those who might be under-represented.

Becoming a Mentor to a Person in an Under-represented Group

We've talked about the savior complex, and that can sometimes come across as condescending. This savior complex can come through in how we are mentoring or sponsoring someone, especially if they are from an under-represented group. In my TEDx talk, I discussed the value of investing versus helping, which is something that's important to establish when people from privileged backgrounds want to support under-represented groups.

Investing in someone suggests that there's going to be a valuable, mutually beneficial relationship eventually, and that there isn't a divide between you and the other person. You're not coming into the relationship thinking you have to save them and that you are better than them, like we discussed when going over the savior complex in chapter five.

This reminds me of a great anecdote. I have a white, Jewish friend who, in the wake of the movement around race relations in 2019, put out a post on social media saying that he was looking to mentor two or three black professionals and for them to contact him if they were interested.

What was interesting was the type of response he received. Some individuals responded with vitriol and others saw where he was coming from. And knowing him and having him as a friend for the last fifteen years, I knew that he was reacting to the scenarios and situations he saw. He was appalled by the racism that he hadn't been aware of, but the way in which he conveyed his desire to make an impact came across as a form of savior complex.

I remember him reaching out to me asking what he did wrong and why people were upset. I knew where he was coming from, but I could also see how people were triggered. Pinpointing black people as the group he wanted to help felt like tokenism, like he was reacting to a situation in a public display. That can feel like someone wants to be seen as a savior, creating a divide where someone is put on a lower pedestal. He was coming from a good place, but it came across as patronizing.

It's really important when working as mentors or sponsors to remember what being an active ally means — we can't assume that we can fix the problem because that's insulting to the journey that individuals from under-represented groups have been on for centuries. When we come in as allies, we get to listen and find that though we might possess some skills that are going to add value to the other person's career, they aren't the only one who's benefiting — it goes both directions.

We can start mentoring those from under-represented groups in small ways by making ourselves more available and interacting with different people within an organization. Welcoming people and inviting them into your space, and having conversations to see where people want to go with their careers can go a long way in making you approachable to all.

The key to reaching out to a potential mentee is to approach the conversation with what the mentee's value to the organization is. This establishes the mutual benefits that you both can get from the mentorship — you aren't handing out a favor or "saving" them. You're authentically making that connection, not trying to be their deity. And many years in the future, or even sooner, you can reap the benefits of the time you invested in this person and the diversity you contributed to.

Your Turn:

Answer the following questions. Be honest with yourself because this work is about self-awareness.

1. Do you have a mentee or mentees?
2. If so, how do they resemble you, and how are they different from you?
3. What's the value of your mentoring relationship to you and your prospective mentee whose background is different from yours?

Take it to Your Team:

Building out a mentoring culture that supports DEI in your organization has to begin with someone. Why not you? Decide to do one of these two things by next Thursday:

1. Option #1: Commit to getting a mentee if you don't already have one. Focus on widening your network and seek a mentee whose background is different from yours in any one of the diversity categories indicated in chapters 1 and 2.
2. Option #2: As part of their development, encourage your direct reports to get a mentor or sponsor. Offer names of potential mentors/sponsors and give the mentors/sponsors a heads up.

CHAPTER NINE

Intersectionality

When looking at your own diversity attributes, you've likely noticed that you sit at the intersection of more than one category within that group. For instance, you might be biracial, multicultural or your family might have incorporated two different faiths into your upbringing.

This is called intersectionality, the idea of a person sitting at the intersection of two or more different subcategories of diversity or associating with multiple groups within one subcategory. This gives someone the ability to understand the experiences or perspectives of two or more different groups. They aren't denying one side of themselves in order to fit into one group. Instead, they celebrate more than one identity and community.

Being biracial, as I just mentioned, is one way someone can be within two categories, or identify with more than one sub-group within a single category. Another way someone can be at the intersection of two identities is by embracing various dimensions of their identity and the cross section between all of those dimensions. For instance, being a woman in the LGBTQIA+ space — your worldview isn't just shaped by the fact that you're a woman. It's shaped by the fact that you're a woman who's also in that community, which is a very different experience than a woman who's heterosexual.

In my first memoir about my journey of being stateless and undocumented, I talk about the struggle I have had at sitting at the intersection being Zambian born, ethnically Congolese from the Democratic Republic of Congo and raised in the US since I was four years old. I felt that I had to deny the other parts of my identity in order to prove that I was American enough to gain a path to citizenship in the US. It wasn't until years after I became a US citizen that I felt that it was safe enough to also refer to myself as Zambian and Congolese.

Understanding intersectionality is more important now than ever before as our world becomes more joined. Groups that might have never "touched" in the past can be connected. For example, people of different socioeconomic groups can follow each other on social media, or there might be more people who appear racially ambiguous and can be mistaken for multiple ethnicities and nationalities.

As we get more exposed to different communities and ideas through travel or social media, we're going to come across more people who sit at the intersection of more than one category. Because of this, we need to understand how intersectionality appears in our work as managers and active allies.

Pitfalls in Understanding Intersectionality

Understanding intersectionality as a concept and as it applies to our teams is another key piece to being an active ally and manager, as well as promoting DEI throughout our organization. It requires a little more work beyond understanding our own biases and trying to mitigate them.

Because of this, there are several pitfalls that managers can run into when they first start taking intersectionality into account.

1) Thinking that people can't embrace more than one identity

It's easy to run the risk of thinking that being part of one group means that you can't be in the other. For instance, someone might not understand how a colleague could be loyal to two completely different cultures or religions.

A reason for this might be American culture is so accustomed to putting labels on people. Being able to put someone into a neat box, or define them in easy terms, creates a sense of safety within ourselves; instead of being an unknown entity, they become something familiar.

But when someone sits at the intersection of two labels, particularly ones that might be seen as mutually exclusive, it becomes a lot more challenging to understand who they are. That can be uncomfortable for many people, including managers. Now there's more work that's required of us to get familiar with that member of our team. It's not that we have to work hard at understanding one part of them, but now we have to try to understand multiple sides of them. We have to spend more time speaking to and connecting with them or making a bigger effort in creating inclusion. Doing so means that we will seldom have the answers and the learning becomes ongoing.

Putting in more effort isn't necessarily what all of us managers want to do, but it can ultimately lead to even better inclusion. By taking the time to understand who's in front of us and who we are speaking to rather than just labeling them based on one part of their narrative, we can make them feel more welcome.

2) Subconsciously forcing their team members to choose one identity over the other

As I mentioned above, sometimes managers can be confused as to how someone could embrace two different identities within the same group or different groups. Because of this, individuals who sit in two categories might feel as if they're being asked to choose one or another because their manager is indirectly expecting them to do so.

For example, a lot of companies might say they're embracing multiculturalism, especially if they're an international corporation. But at the end of the day, a lot of workplaces I've observed really want people to assimilate to American culture and frame their business from that point of view. This might appear as companies not considering time zones outside of the US when scheduling meetings or creating important events during another country's holiday season.

Connecting all of the different regions of your company and creating a team that gels takes a lot of work, just as getting to know all of the layers of someone's diversity. That leads into the next issue that can surface when exploring intersectionality.

3) Not seeing the opportunities that exploring intersectionality can bring

Getting to know the ways in which your team members sit at the intersection of multiple identities or categories will take longer than just getting to know the aspects of that person individually and, as I've mentioned, that takes a lot more work that some managers may want.

However, doing this work can be a great opportunity for growth. When we go above and beyond to understand how someone's identity is unique, we further increase their feelings of belonging. As I've mentioned, that boosts productivity, efficiency, and growth for not just that one person, but the entire team.

This kind of growth just requires us to be willing to listen and ask open-ended questions, even though it can be intimidating and uncomfortable but, as I've mentioned in previous chapters, being uncomfortable is a part of growing at work. This doesn't mean asking questions to make the individual feel further "othered." What it entails is acknowledging the diversity that each individual brings to the team and building trust so that person feels included. Assuming that they feel included can be damaging because it's based on your point of privilege.

Intersectionality and Management

Now that we know how we can make mistakes around intersectionality, how can we approach it and incorporate it into how we manage our teams.

1) We have to let people self-identify rather than assuming they're part of a monolith

Letting people self-identify clearly connects to how we approach being active allies and managers — rather than being the narrator of someone else's story and making assumptions, we have to listen to them and amplify their voice.

Like we discussed in chapter seven on tokenism, one person doesn't speak for their entire community or see everything in the same way. One woman isn't representative of all women, and one man isn't representative of all men. Likewise, two people from the Latinx community won't automatically think the same way and, if there was a chance that they did, their experiences combined wouldn't represent the totality of the Latinx community.

When we understand this, it lessens the pressure and burden of always knowing what to say. The reason we avoid discussion, particularly around race, is because we are afraid of getting it wrong and offending someone. I have often been asked whether the correct term is Latinx, Hispanic, or Latino. My response is that all three labels represent different groups of people with different histories. If you are looking for a general term to refer to the group, then it's valuable to understand why Latinx is the most relevant term.

However, not everyone of Hispanic or Latinx descent will refer to themselves as Latinx. The best thing to do is to ask when you are unclear. Reaching the level of confidence when navigating discussions around diversity requires recognition that since most of us sit at the cross-section of race, ethnicity, nationality and so forth, we are better off letting people define themselves.

Also, two different people from the same background might have a completely different take on issues concerning their race, and one person's experiences shouldn't be conflated with another. For instance, Candice Owens, a Black political commentator who speaks on issues concerning race, might believe that racism against Black people no longer exists. Just because she happens to be Black and feels that way, doesn't make her statement more accurate.

No group is a monolith. When we understand that, we can get to know the individual, listen to their story, and make them feel included.

2) We have to perform due diligence to see where there are more opportunities for growth in our team's diversity

Even if we understand the three layers of diversity that I've outlined in this book, we still need to go beyond that to see where we might need more representation or more attention.

Finding where we might need more representation isn't looking at just one layer of diversity by itself. And it's also not about looking at all of the layers individually without seeing how they intersect. If people's identities span multiple groups, you have to understand the different categories that can exist within each of their categories. For instance, if we're thinking about nationality, we can't just assume that everyone on your US-based team solely identifies as American. You have to think, "What are all the other nationalities that people on my team could identify with?"

If we're analyzing our metrics of DEI, we can look beyond individual categories, like sex or gender or race, and dive deeper into the layers of what we are looking at. It's easy to look and say, "In our offices, we have a 50/50 split between men and women." But what happens when you look at the breakdown of gender by race? You might find that of the 50% women, only 3% are Black and Latinx, 12% are Asian and the rest are white. By diving deeper into the data, it's easier to identify the root cause of a gap in diversity.

3) We have to think about what diversity truly means

Addressing intersectionality encourages us to really unpack what diversity means and not support only one area of it. It's easy for us to <u>say</u> our teams are diverse by pointing at our diversity of thought or diversity of appearance, but that can't be the only thing that matters.

By seeing someone's many layers of diversity, and more importantly, how they interact to create that person's unique point of view, we can better understand that person and coach them in the way that brings out their fullest potential.

Intersectionality is a necessary part of understanding DEI, one that will become increasingly more important as our world becomes more and more intertwined. We can be proactive and ensure that we see everyone's unique story, rather than trying to label them for our own comfort.

Your Turn:

1. Recall a time when you made an assumption about a person based on a diversity category they belonged to and they turned out to be the exact opposite of what you expected?

Take it to Your Team:

1. Reach out to your Human Resources team and ask to look at DEI attributes for your team across three or more categories (e.g., gender/race/age). This cross-section of data offers more predictive and descriptive analysis.

DEI is About Being Human

After the death of George Floyd, one of my friends who happens to be a white woman told me about the Zoom call her team had to discuss the national response to racial injustice. Her manager essentially put the only black woman on their team on the spot to come up with answers about what was going on, as if she were an expert just because they have the same skin color. My friend asked me, "Martine, what do you think I should do? I just felt really bad seeing that happen."

I told her, "Let's reposition this. If there was a national conversation about gender relations and you were put on the spot as the only woman on a team of men, just as your black co-worker was, what would you want? How would you want someone to exercise empathy towards you? Would you want someone to reach out to you?"

She told me that she would like to be reached out to, but on a one-on-one basis, just to see if there was a way they could support her. It was perfect — she answered her own question. It doesn't have to be more complicated than that. She practiced empathy and understanding, skills she already had.

Sometimes the belief that DEI is complex comes from mistakenly conflating it with Equal Employment Opportunity laws and policies. Managers might avoid talking about diversity in general in fear that they'll say or do the wrong thing, which, as we know, isn't the way forward.

An analogy to understand the difference between EEO laws and DEI could be something like child support. Say a man is divorcing his spouse and he's legally required to pay $1500 a month at a minimum to his ex-spouse for their child. If the man just pays the $1500 a month to meet the legal requirement, that's similar to a company just doing enough to meet EEO requirements. But DEI is more like him giving extra in months when he has more income, even though he's not required to by law.

Following EEO doesn't make a company great, it just makes it compliant. DEI can take a company from good to great. We get an opportunity to find people who look or think differently from us, which adds so much value to the workplace.

Yes, it's true that it won't happen overnight, and we won't know absolutely everything. But we can make an effort to understand, listen, ask open-ended questions and be empathetic to someone else's story. It's about validation and inclusion, not agreement or exclusion. You don't have to step out of a conversation or compromise your desires or beliefs to be a good ally.

Another way to understand how straightforward the foundation of DEI can be is to think of it as a natural extension of the skills you have as a manager. When you think about it, you're focused on hiring, promotions, performance management, salary adjustments, motivating your team, and generally helping them reach their best. We can also motivate people by listening to their story and validating their experiences, or hinder that upward trajectory by tokenizing them or overlooking microaggressions. All of that is connected to DEI.

So, when we think about DEI as an extension of being a good manager, we can understand how to implement it. DEI doesn't have to be about our studies in Critical Race Theory in graduate school; that's what we have the experts for. We can start by asking questions that we'd ask ourselves in regards to our management practices as a whole. For instance, where are we lacking? Or, where do we have the opportunity to widen our perspective?

To further simplify what DEI really is, we can break it down into the ABCs — active listening and avoiding avoidance, being empathetic through validation, and lastly, coaching.

Active Listening and Avoiding Avoidance

When managers encounter anything related to diversity, we don't have to fear that it's going to compromise our ability to succeed. We can think of it as an opportunity to ask the people on our team, within our company, or within our network questions — how and where are things the same? Where do we have the opportunity to create more inclusion? How can we widen our candidate pool or how can we change?

And when we ask those questions or engage in DEI conversations, we avoid avoidance. As the workplace continues to become more diverse, these conversations will become inevitable. It behooves us to do the work and face the issues in an empathetic, straightforward way.

Just because it doesn't feel comfortable or natural, doesn't mean it's not necessary. As long as no one's safety is compromised, we ought to encourage our teams and our organizations to discover the potential that DEI offers.

Being Empathetic Through Validation

In order to validate someone, we really have to listen to understand. We can't listen and point out where they're flawed in their thinking, or where they're wrong, or whether or not we agree.

Validation disarms people and allows them to start sharing and opening up to you. It doesn't mean that you automatically agree. Being empathetic through validating just means that you let someone know that you hear them, and that you're trying your best to understand where they're coming from.

Coaching

Like I said, a lot of DEI efforts boil down to the fundamentals of being a manager. Coaching is one of those basics that we can use to incorporate DEI into our day-to-day work. Stop trying to fix situations or become a savior.

Instead, empower the person by collaborating with them. That's what we'd do in any other situation — we would delegate tasks and coach them through any difficulties they might have. So, we already know how to have courageous conversations outside of DEI if someone disagrees with us, or if they're having conflict with someone else on the team.

We already have all the skills we need. The core of it is listening and not avoiding the issue, as I mentioned above. We don't have to know all the answers. Instead, we have to be empathetic, transparent, and willing to learn.

There's lots of jargon, euphemisms and statistics that can support your DEI efforts. But at the end of the day, it's really as simple as putting yourself in their shoes, or looking at things from their lens, and thinking about how you'd like to be treated in that situation, just like my friend on the Zoom call from the beginning of the chapter. DEI is accessible to all of us. That's why this book is called the ABCs of Diversity — it's as simple as being human.

Made in the USA
Las Vegas, NV
10 March 2022

45431022R00079